Policymaking and Development Strategies for Local Governments in Nigeria

Chima Imoh (Ph.D., Public Policy

and Leadership)

Heritage Publishing Company

_____

Houston, United States of America

Heritage Publishing Company,

7447 Harwin Drive,

Houston, TX 77036.

Library of Congress control Number:

Imoh, Chima

Policymaking and Development Strategies for Local Governments in Nigeria/Chima Imoh

P.cm.-(policymaking, development and local administration)

ISBN-978-0985479220

1. Democracy-development-policymaking. 2. Nigeria-local Governments- strategic policymaking. I. Title. II. Series

Printed in the United States of America

PREFACE

The purpose of this book is to highlight prevalent democratic principles and how they can impact on public policy formulation and projects development in local governments in Nigeria. The book explores the impacts of democratic theories as they relate to the new perspectives for public administration, especially at the local government levels. Much of the discussions in this book pertain to the democratic and policymaking principles that could engineer effective and sustainable public policy formulation within the local administration machineries. The book, therefore, focuses on the use of democratic institutions as tools for localized governance.

The earlier tendency of thinking of public policies as the result of the decision-making processes of governments does seem to be losing its potency. This book strives to marshal out concise and intense logic and reasoning to show that collaborative, representative, deliberative, and participatory democratic orientation are all relevant to modern day policy making. The deliberative and collaborative perspectives of democracy do also address the problems of today's policymaking with regard to creating and enhancing citizen participation in governance.

The book also uses these democratic perspectives to design the corrective measures that are needed for the successful policy formulation and implementation in local government administrations in Nigeria. By identifying the factors that have led to the failures of public policy and service delivery in Nigeria, this book develops the problem solution steps for the country's public policy processes in local government administration.

Essentially, the book seeks to relate these perspectives to citizen empowerment and participation in public policymaking and service delivery at the grassroots levels. Public policies formulation during a democratic dispensation is usually more representative, participatory, and hence more sustainable. By analyzing these perspectives, their effects on the policymaking in local governments of Nigeria become more appreciated.

Discussed in this book is the contemporary orientation of policymaking as it relates and creates new roles for public administrators. This book illustrates the significance of the various democratic approaches and discusses the challenges public policymaking in local in governance. The importance of deliberative democracy, democratic renewal, and citizen participation in governance is emphasized as an important normative concern in public policy formulation.

Consensus exists among public administration scholars that partnerships between nonprofit, business and government sectors are becoming more pronounced in most countries as the societal problems become more complex and difficult for the individual sectors. Public policy practitioners and public administrators are increasingly realizing the benefits of collaboration. This book, hence, explores the alternative non-governmental means of influencing policymaking and delivering public services.

The book is also aimed at creating the developmental strategy that would offer avenues for achieving meaningful partnerships between local government agencies and neighborhood councils/ development unions/town unions under a metropolitan environment. This is based on citizen participation that focuses on the significance of interactive processes in building the trust among participants, and creating understanding and agreement. The book presents a model of citizen participation, designed to forge neighborhood councils and local government agencies together in a collaborative partnership. This model also offers a way for citizens and public administrators to overcome obstacles that prevent the creation of government-citizen relationships.

Chima Imoh, Ph. D.

ABOUT THE AUTHOR

Chima Imoh has a degree in Geodetic Engineering and a master's degree in international management. He holds a doctorate degree in Public policy and Administration, specializing in public management and leadership. Dr Imoh is a member of the National Honor Society for Public Affairs and Administration, United States of America. The author has lectured and worked in public institutions in the United States and in Africa. Dr Chima Imoh is the author of the book, Cultural Competence for Global Management and a co-author of the book, *Competence for Public Administration,* edited by Dr Susan T. Gooden and Dr Kris Major.

CONTENTS

Chapter 1: The Classical Theories of
Democracy..1

Chapter 2: Contemporary Practices of
Democracy..7

Chapter 3: Elements and Concepts of
Public Policymaking......................14

Chapter 4: The Processes of Public
Policymaking..............................21

Chapter 5: The Faces of Public
Policymaking..............................25

Chapter 6: The Politics of Public
Policymaking..............................34

Chapter 7: Problems of Policymaking in
Nigeria's Local Governments............41

Chapter 8: Public Policymaking under
Democratic Governance...................46

Chapter 9: Development under
Democratic Governance...................52

Chapter 10: Local Government
Administration under Federalism.........59

Chapter 11: The New Trends in Local Government Administration................62

Chapter 12: New Roles for Local Government Administrators...............66

Chapter 13: The Challenges of Policymaking in Local Government Administration..73

Chapter 14: Improving the Policy Processes in Local Governance...........80

Chapter15: Development Unions/Neighbourhood Associations as Development Partners.....................87

Chapter 16: Strategic Planning in Local Government Administration................91

Chapter 17: Example of Governance by Collaboration: Waste Management Strategies for local Governments..........97

APPENDIXES......................107-108

ENDNOTES...........................109

Chapter 1

The Classical Theories of Democracy

Democracy can be defined as the institutional arrangement for arriving at political decisions in which individuals acquire the power to decide by means of competitive struggle for other peoples' votes[1]. The very essence of democratic governance consists of the absolute sovereignty of the majority; with the legislature been the embodiment of this absolute power and supremacy[2]. Democratic governance, therefore, involve free debates and legislative procedures, subject to public scrutiny and criticism[3]. Democracy has, thus, increasingly become the only basis of legitimate government; and the idea has caught on that regime is legitimate only when it is based on the will of the people[4]. Generally, most democratic principles encourage representation, basic rights, and the sovereignty of the people.

The concept of democracy is fundamentally hinged on the proposition that political sovereignty originates with the citizens[5]. Democracy, therefore, bears such time-cherished values as the equality of the citizenry, the responsiveness and accountability of the government to the governed, the transparency of government actions and services, and the accessibility of all to government programs and services.

Democracy cannot, however, be genuinely defined from only one perspective. Essentially, there is no democratic theory, but rather, democratic theories[6]. The theoretical concepts of democracy come in many different shapes and sizes and that there is by no means a consensus on which strand is preferable[7]. Although there have been much scholarly arguments regarding the perspective of democracy that would best bring these values to fruition, democracy can be analyzed from the perspective of three theories of competition, egalitarianism and deliberation.

The Competitive Theory
Led by the 19th century Austrian-American economist and political scientist Joseph Alois Schumpeter (1883- 1950), competitive theorists have an economic perspective of democracy as a free competition for free vote in the political realm. From this free market-style orientation, it therefore, follows that most forms of

anticompetitive behaviors are to be expected and tolerated in democracies[8]. This perspective suggests that, given the nature of those who seek political power, any attempt to create more perfect competition in politics is bound to fail[9]; and it is therefore, unrealistic to expect perfect competition in a democratic system. The perspective here is that the free market-style of competition is necessary for the democratic system.

For the Schumpeterian scholars, however, the promotion of this competition is of lesser importance; rather, the interest should be on preserving the integrity of the ballot or preventing its corruption[10]. A democratic system cannot, therefore, be considered genuine if the ballot is compromised, or preferences are coerced[11]. This perspective tends to indicate that protecting the votes of the citizens as well as promoting the enabling environment for free and fair competitions among contending parties is more paramount.

The Schumpeterian scholars, however, argue that political issues are so remote from the daily lives of the ordinary people that they cannot make sound judgments nor have informed opinions on public policies[12]. The perception is that public discussion of measures under consideration is not essential to this concept of democracy[13], hence shutting the door on deliberative concept of democracy. The fallout of this theoretical outlook is that massive political participation is undesirable and that the electoral masses are incapable of political participation other than voting for their leaders[14].

An apparent flaw of this Schumpeterian perspective is that political competition requires only electoral competition[15]. So long as two parties or candidates are involved in a political contest, the assumption becomes that competition has been satisfied[16]. Stretched further, it becomes quite acceptable to have political systems in which two parties dominate; others cannot effectively compete, or are completely excluded. This theory is obviously not in consonance with the realities of modern day democratic principles.

The Egalitarian Theory
The egalitarian theorists led by Robert Dahl have argued that democracy is not about the realization of majority will through democratic accountability and representation; but rather about a pluralist society in which multitude of minorities seek to advance their goals through both electoral and non-electoral means[17]. This school of thought insists that the essence of democracy should be the promotion and protection of fundamental rights and the enthronement of an egalitarian society, placing more emphasis on basic rights as the substantive core of procedural democracy[18].

This perspective contends that the value of democracy lies, not in representation, but in the protection of rights of the citizens to hold officials accountable or throw them out of office[19]. The postulation here is that democracy is more about legitimacy and acceptability of leaders than they are about representation of the will of the majority[20]. The "democratic measure" of a society should, therefore, be based on such indices as basic human rights, supremacy of the people's sovereignty and its egalitarianism.

The Deliberative Theory
Deliberative democracy stresses the creation of institutional contexts and practices that encourage and promote collaborative planning between citizens and government[21]. The idea of deliberative democracy focuses on the free political discussion, open legislative deliberations, and the pursuit of a common good[22]. This concept of deliberative democracy represents the ideal political autonomy based on the practical reasoning of the citizens[23].

The superiority of this perspective rests on the fact that, in a democratic system in which citizens are politically equal and are bound to disagree, deliberative democracy demands that each citizen should be able to explain what he or she believes[24]. From this reasoning, since decision-making would require that citizens who deliberate must provide justification for the positions they take, the quality of debates become enhanced[25]. The deliberative exchanges can also lead participants to correct flaws in their analysis; make them move from fixated positions and explore new alternatives, which, until then, were unknown to them[26]. From its own dynamics, deliberation compels participants to adopt particular modes of formulating their demands and induces a specific way of assessing them[27]. This unique characteristic of deliberative school enhances the quality and acceptance of public policies.

This strain of democracy is a positive alternative to the competitive theory in which a majority can decide the government's action without recourse, or even justifying its position to the minority. The main problem in the practice of the deliberative theory is that citizens do not often have any incentives to deliberate or to inform themselves in a manner that could enable them develop informed opinions [28].

Chapter 2

Contemporary Practices of Democracy

Democracy has become an attractive form of governance because its principles embrace human needs and desires, and can, in reality, often deliver them[1]. Democracy starts with the citizens as the pillars of the democratic framework is embedded in the rights of the citizens and the ability of the state to guarantee equal rights of the citizens through constitutional and legal processes[2]. A strong democracy is operationally definable as one in which political participation is fully competitive, the executive recruitment is elective, and the constraints on the executive are substantial[3].

The core values of democratic governance are hinged on the keys principles of liberty and equality, manifesting as the rule of law and sovereignty of the people [4]. The rule of law is practiced through the legal values of civil, property, political, and minority rights, that in turn, guarantee individual freedoms and protections[5]. On its part, the sovereignty of the people is practiced through such institutional values as accountability, representation, constraints and participation[6]. Quinine democracies will, therefore, have institutionalize procedures for open, competitive, and deliberative political participation, choosing and replacing chief executives in open, competitive elections, imposing structural checks and balances on the power of the chief executive[7].

Democracy can also be conceived as three essential, interdependent elements: (i) the presence of institutions and procedures through which citizens can express preferences about alternative policies and leaders, (ii) the existence of institutionalized constraints on the exercise of power by the executive, (iii) the guarantee of civil liberties to all citizens in their daily lives and acts of political participation[8]. The rule of law, systems of checks and balances, freedom of press and other aspects of plural democracy are manifestations of these three broad principles[9]. The democratic ideal in and itself seeks to guarantee equality and basic freedom; the empowerment of the citizens, resolution of disagreement through peaceful means, and to enthrone political, social and renewals without disruption[10]. Essentially, the practice of democracy offers popular control over the elected leaders, equal rights and liberties, political freedom, and freedom from wants, the rule of law, justice, and security[11].

Essentially, a democratic state espouses and supports such rights as freedoms of expression, worship, movement, assembly, and from want. A state or regime is, hence, not democratic by calling it so or by merely embracing such institutions of democracy as the legislature and judiciary, as is the case in quasi-democracies or electoral authoritarianism.

Citizen Participation in Democracies

A series of positions regarding the relevance of direct citizen's participation to the values of democracy and the effectiveness of the policymaking process have always been canvassed. According to Jean Jacques Rousseau (1712-1778), the health of a polity is   depended on active citizen participation and involvement in all aspects of governance[12]. A robust and healthy democracy is, however, only as possible as the active participation of the citizens in public life[13]. Citizenship participation is, therefore, the cornerstone of democracy[14].

In the democratic society, therefore, citizens have a fundamental right to participate[15]. This is essential because, citizen participation brings enormous values to the policymaking process.

The advocacy of greater citizen participation is important for a variety of reasons: to promote democracy, build trust, increase transparency, enhance accountability, build social capital, reduce conflict, ascertain priorities, promote legitimacy, and cultivate understanding, or advance fairness, and justice[16].

Essentially, democracy requires some degree of citizen participation in governance; otherwise, participatory democracy would remain an elusive ideal[17]. The challenge is how to concretize the concept and make it more practicable. For instance, direct participation enhances and protects the rights of the electoral and ethnic minorities. Direct participation becomes more relevant to the extent that it is able to extend effective power to these disadvantaged groups in such ways that enhance and protect their rights.

Although it could be granted that it is quite difficult, albeit impossible to create participation for the entire citizenry, a degree of equality in political participation is symbolically important for a legitimate political system[18]. Moreover, some minimal level of participation is necessary to maintain stability in a political community[19]. Autocratic and democratic regimes both regulate participation but in different ways. Autocratic regimes do so by channeling participation through a single structure (such as one party) that imposes sharp limits on the diversity of opinion; in contrast, democratic regimes allow groups to compete nonviolently for political influence[20].

Political Competition in Democracies

In the book, Democracy and Development, Przeworski, Alvarez, Cheibub, and Limongi (2000) argued that democracy is the system of governance where government offices are filled through contested elections. They contended that organized competition and elections, through the power of the vote validates the basic concept of modern democracy[21]. As with freedom of speech and freedom of association, political competition, determined through free and fair elections is also a central component of democracy[22].

This political competition, which is consequent upon free and fair elections, is the "life of democracy" and "meaningful political competition requires that there be opposition parties, waiting in the wings, criticizing the government and offering voters potential alternative"[23]. In democratic countries, therefore, opposition parties thrive, elections are free and fair are held, and ruling parties are sometimes voted out of power.

Democracy, therefore, leads to higher levels of satisfaction with the government, because the inherent political competition creates a balance between the politician, supposed to supply good governance and the citizens who demand good governance[24]. These public goods manifest in forms of enhancement public safety and rule of law, protection of civil and human rights, creation of sustainable economic opportunities for the citizens, control of corruption educational attainment, life expectancy, and income per capita.

Without this credible threat of replacements through elections, however, elected officials have fewer incentives to provide public goods[25]. Being democratic, therefore, means welcoming the existence of opposition parties, and letting them organize and campaign freely against the ruling party. The presence of credible opposition, therefore, ushers in accountability. This political accountability ensures the responsiveness and accountability of the government to the governed, the transparency of government actions and services, and the accessibility of all to government programs, and services should be of primary concern. It is, therefore, noteworthy that greater checks on politicians and greater accountability to citizens are both indicators by which a distinction can be made between democratic regimes from authoritarian regimes[26]. Moreover, the tendency to convert public resources is discouraged, and welfare-enhancing public services encouraged when governments are made more politically responsive and accountable[27].

Specifically, modern democratic theory conceptualizes a democratic system as the polity that affords its citizen the opportunity to replace their political representation through regularly scheduled, competitive and open elections[28]. Only an opposition that has the potential to win an election and form a new government can provide a strong external incentive for the incumbent government to act in the interest of the citizens[29].

Chapter 3

Elements and Concepts of Public Policymaking

The key values of any country's government are usually spelt in its constitution. The values that have evolved from the constitutional provisions of most nations include equality of the citizenry, the responsiveness and accountability of the government to the governed, the transparency of government actions and services, and the accessibility of all to government programs and services.

The operating principles of the public policy process are similarly concepts like justice, equity, and fairness. These values presume that all people are created equal, and should be so treated; and hence, in its ideal sense, all citizens should be guaranteed the same rights and services from the government. These equality values, which developed into the concept of common good (otherwise called public interest) and equity in public affairs is necessary to make public policies more acceptable to the majority of the people in the society. Although there are no quantitative measures for these concepts of justice, equity, and fairness, the society does seem to have some idea about how well the public policy process is performing along these lines[1].

Public Policy Definitions
The definitions of public policies are wide and varied. Public policy is the course of actions made by a public body, as the government, and is representative of the interests of the larger society[2]. Public policy is a political system's response to the demands arising from its environment [3]. Public policy can also be described as that pattern of government activity on some topic that has a purpose or goal and is hence, a purposeful and goal-oriented behavior rather than a random behavior [4].

Public policies are developed by government institutions and officials through the political process and are distinct from other kinds of policies because they result from actions of legitimate authorities in the political system[5]. Public policy can also be viewed as a government's expressed intention that is backed by a sanction that is meant to encourage obedience to the policy[6]. Another description of public policy is whatever government chooses to do or not to do; and must also include what government chooses not to do because government inaction on particular issues can have as much an impact on the society as government's action[7].

Concisely, any course of action taken collectively by the society or by a legitimate representative of the society to address a specific societal problem or public concern is public policy[8]. These courses of action must, however, reflect the interests of the society or a particular segment of the society[9].

Public problems
Public problems are those issues of utmost concerns to the citizens or residents of a municipality. The key criteria that should guide the policy analyst in identifying policy problems is if it affects a substantial number of people with broad effects and have consequences for all including those not directly involved[10]. Another criterion is whether anything can be done about the problem. If nothing can be done about the problem, then it is not a policy problem. It follows that conditions could only be considered as problems if we believe we should do something about them[11].

Customarily, there have been conflicts over the causation of policy problems. The sources of these conflicts include the differences in our values, the differences in origins and trace; and the differences in our political ideologies. Differences in the information available to us, differences in our education and experiences also play significant roles. The entities involved in identifying policy problems include interest groups, legislators, the executive, and the citizenry. Such international organizations as the World trade organization, World health Organization (WHO), United Nations' Educational, Scientific and Cultural Organization (UNESCO), United Nations' Organization (UNO), and other international organizations also identify policy problems.

Citizen sovereignty

The vote is the ultimate power citizens have in a democratic system; hence, citizens should have sovereignty over the public policy process[12]. An issue that seems to undermine citizens' sovereignty is that most people are not usually interested in public issues, especially when such issues do not directly concern them. People who do not participate thus sacrifice their sovereign and power to the minority that show interest in political life, and thus participate actively to the formulation of public policy for the entire society[13].

Public Goods and services

Public goods and services are by their nature necessary and available to everyone, whether or not they have helped to pay for them[14]. This unique nature of public goods and services seems to be the reason public policy decisions have to be made through the public policy process[15]. Public goods and services are indivisible into individual units to meet individual preferences[16]. This indivisibility gives these goods their public character and if people would at all have them, they must be enjoyed them roughly in the same amount[17]. Property rights do not apply here because these goods and services are not owned individually[18]. The delivery of these public goods and services is the main thrust of public administration. The value that public administrators should bring to bear on the society is by working to ensure the accessibility of services to the citizenry in timely and effective manners. Although it is tenable for the government to provide the enabling environment to equal access to public goods, the lofty goal of ensuring equal enjoyment is more difficult to attain.

Public interest

Public interests could be viewed from perspectives as; (i) the aggregation, weighing and balancing of a number of special interests,

(ii) the outcome of free and open competition of interested parties who have to compromise their differences to arrive at a common course of action (ii) and (iii) the sum of all private interests in the community, balanced for the common good[19]. Although it is not possible to provide a universally accepted or objective definition of the concept of public interest, some schools of thought believe that whatever results from the political struggle over policy issues is the public interest[20]. A decision is in public interest if it serves the ends of the whole public, rather than those of some sector of the public, and if it incorporates all interests and concepts of value, which are acceptable to the society[21]. Moreover, if the interested parties have had ample opportunity to express their views, the outcome of the process is therefore, public interest by definition[22].

Diversity in Value Systems

The political process is a complex amalgam of power and influence that involves many actors who, in pursuing different interests, try to persuade, and influence others to achieve their objectives[23]. People pursue their own interests through the political process based on the values they hold relative to the objectives sought collectively[24]. Often, these interests are contrasting and contending. Worse still, sometimes, there is no common value system that values can be translated[25]. Values are "strongly held preferences or standards that guide the conduct of people" [26]. Values can help us determine between right and wrong, and can help us to set priorities[27]. Values are important for individuals, organizations, and governments to have, but they are useless unless practiced[28]. To be constructively relevant, however, values must be transformed into action. Usually an individual has an internal set of standards, values and principles that guide one's everyday decisions. More often than not, this lack of common value system makes effective legislation and resource allocation more problematic.

Determining how contending parties can agree and cooperate on the same goals could be difficult. However, there is quite a possibility that conflict and cooperation can hobnob as bedfellows. After all, two parties may agree on goals but disagree strongly on how to meet those goals. Any conflicts arising from diversified value system could be made productive when it leads to resolution and to a new understanding of how the parties can mutually achieve joint needs. Generally, the existence of this diverse value system makes value conflicts in the public policy process to be more pronounced, thereby creating some measure of ethical dilemmas for the public administrator[29].

Chapter 4

The Processes of Public Policymaking

The previous views of some politicians and public administrators that providing the platform for citizen participation amounted to empowering the people at the expense of administrative and political powers were quite misguided. This perspective remains faulty because encouraging citizen participation and collaboration in the public management process are win-win games that should constitute the backbone of public administration[1]. The citizens could bring their particular knowledge and skills into the delivery and management of public services and by so doing; improve the quality and effectiveness of policy implementation[2]. As responsive signs of care and willingness to work with citizens, it is also important for public officers and professional in government to meet citizens on their own ground[3].

Public Agenda Setting

Public policy agenda are those collections of topics and issues with respect to which public policy may be formulated[4]. There are many problems and concerns that various people in a society want to be acted upon; but only those considered important enough to receive serious attention from the policymakers constitute public policy agenda[5]. Public policy is the list of subjects to which public administrators are paying serious attention at any given time[6]. The existence of public policy agenda is thus found in the collective actions and judgment of the society, concerns and actions of the interest groups, congressional legislatures, and cases brought into consideration by the Supreme Court[7].

The agenda setting for public problems usually elicits a measure of uncertainties. The uncertainty over policy goals usually arises from the dynamics of agenda setting in policy formulation. The activities of political and interest groups sometimes make it difficult for policymakers to narrow the goals and objectives of a policy to specifics. The more obtuse the goals and objectives are, the more the possibility of wider acceptance; and hence, the higher the potentials of elevating them to legislative or administrative agenda.

Public Policy Adoption
The policy theories that govern public policy adoption include the political systems theory, institutionalism, rational-choice theory, and group theory, and elite theory. These theories are needed to guide the study of public policies, facilitate public policy communication, and also offer explanations for public policies[8]. The most prevalent of the policy theories are the group theory in which public policies are shaped and formulated based on group interests. The equity theory approach to public policies should be more commonly applied because it ensures greater fairness. Fairness in the delivery of public services is governed by the principle that each citizen regardless of economic resources or personal traits has the right to receive equal treatment by the political system.

Public Policy Implementation and Evaluation
The policy tools, which help decision makers in establishing the criteria for evaluating policy options, can be grouped into broad categories: technical feasibility of the option, its economic and financial possibility, its political viability, and its administrative "operatability". The technical feasibility criterion would address such issues regarding the ability of the policy outcomes to meet the desired objectives. The emphasis in this assessment approach is on the effectiveness and adequacy of the option[9]. The

economic and financial possibility criterion analyzes such issues as the cost and benefit of the program, economic efficiency, and cost effectiveness and in some cases, its profitability.

The most worrisome of all criteria is its political viability. Politics introduces situation, which are not measurable but only sentimental. This in turn, distorts the evaluation criteria because issues of appropriateness, responsiveness, and equity are usually difficult to evaluate. Finally, the administrative machineries of governments are charged with the responsibility of implementing public programs. Hence, even if all the other criteria are available, the ability of the administrative machinery to deliver the policy becomes a major issue. All these evaluation criteria usually invite tons of public analysis, debates, and activism.

Public policy Analysis

Policy analysis is a set of techniques that seeks to answer the question of what the probable effects of a policy will be before they occur. All policy analysis involves the application of systematic research techniques to the formulation, execution and evaluation of public policy to create a more rational or optimal administrative system[10]. A good deal of public debates and participation are involved in the analysis of determining if a project is achieving its goals.

Chapter 5

The Faces of Public Policymaking

The processes of public policymaking have multiple dimensions. These would include the roles of the citizen, the public administrators, and governments in the process. Some scholars have argued that citizens are better served through representation, whereas others posit that such is more effective through direct participation. The other perspectives of citizen deliberation and collaboration are, however, the more effective and participatory perspective to public administration at the municipal government level.

The means and modes of public policy debates, the ways public policies become formulated, and the implementation of public policies have much impact on how public problems are analyzed and confronted by a society. Although public policy making bears multiple faces, participatory and collaborative dimensions of policy making are most relevant to modern public administration, and have become the hallmark of today's policymaking process. This is because public service delivery has evolved from the era in which citizens were treated as mere consumers, to clients, and now as collaborators.

Different from its traditional top-bottom role of policymaking and implementation, modern public policy has assumed different perspectives. The modern policymaking process today has become all-pervading and more complex. Collaboration, consensus building, deliberation, and dialogue are emerging trends toward working out solutions to public problems. Consensus building enables stakeholders build unified fronts on actions necessary to address public problems or issues of mutual concern.

Public policy as a representative process
Proponents of representative in policy making, otherwise regarded as indirect citizen participation, argue that it has such benefits as protecting the citizens from the dangers of direct participation. They posit that it "buffers them from uninformed public opinion, prevents the

tyranny of the majority, and as a check on corruption"[1]. Another argument by proponents is that public officials are in better positions than the citizens to devote the time and efforts necessary for fostering informed opinions. They also argue that citizens do not have the time and interest to deliberate for the purpose of developing informed public judgments[2] and that the complexities of the modern society exclude direct citizen participation as a realistic option for public policymaking and administration[3].

Contrary to the views held by these proponents of representative policy making, the scale and diversity of Nigerian society present serious challenges to the possibility that elected representatives can, in any real sense, be reflective and representative of the constituency diversities[4]. This because, as social and management theorist, Mary Parker Follett (1868-1933) pointed out in the early part of the twentieth century; the inadequacy of representative government is that it lacks the capacity for empowering the citizens in matters that concern them directly[5]. Governance should, therefore, be restructured in such a manner as to integrate the grassroots representations; consisting of citizens in their neighborhoods deliberating among themselves[6].

Public Policy as a Participatory process
Citizen participation has immense effect on the

political and administrative processes of a society. In a democratic society, citizenship is the cornerstone and citizens, therefore, have a fundamental right to participate; thereby promoting the effectiveness of public policymaking[7]. A healthy democracy is only as possible as the active participation of the citizens in public life[8]. Robert Putnam, political scientist and Harvard professor of public policy advocates greater citizen participation for a variety of reasons: to promote democracy, build trust, increase transparency, enhance accountability, and build social capital[9]. Other reasons are: to reduce conflict, ascertain priorities, promote legitimacy, and cultivate understanding, or advance fairness, and justice[10]. Moreover, participation has the value of making the citizen aware of the views of others, more accepting of the decisions and that the individual ideally becomes less selfish if he or she participates in decisions[11].

From the perspective of social change and citizen empowerment in public policy making process, citizen participation is an effective tool that also enhances policy outcomes[12]. This citizen empowerment could also serve as helping tool for preventing the further deteriorating of the much-needed public trust[13].

Direct participation becomes more relevant to the extent that it could extend effective power to these disadvantaged groups in such ways that enhance and protect their rights. Participation is only valuable to the extent that it redistributes power in such a manner that the have-nots are deliberately involved in future decision-making processes[14].

All said, for the societies that espouse democratic values, citizen participation in governance should be advocated whether or not it results in more efficient or effective public policies[15]. Democratic practices, shaped by the public sector through the organization of citizens in collaborative forums may be more inclusive and effective than acts of traditional political participation because with the pressures for improved governance, citizen participation in the decision-making processes of the government receives more and better attention[16].

The overarching and distinguishing character of the administrative machineries of the state usually creates barriers to citizen participation in governance[17]. Creating, developing, and nurturing citizen participation within the context of the administrative apparatuses of the state is, therefore, a significant challenge[18]. Against the background of the usual practice of citizen representation, there is the need to evaluate the redefined roles of public officials and citizens. Rather than treating citizens as clients or consumers, they should be treated as partners and equal stakeholders in the policymaking process.

Public policy as a deliberative process

The deliberative public participation goes beyond the individualistic roles of citizens as traditional voters or customers who delight in the services designed by others. Deliberative public participation tends to envision citizens helping to develop policy through peer-to-peer deliberation.

Modern policymaking process today has become all-pervading and more complex, and there is a growing tendency by public agencies to recognize that they cannot solve problems alone and that developing complete solution depends on collaboration[19]. The exchange of ideas between participants in deliberative forums makes the deliberative process an ideal format for policymaking[20]. The deliberative processes of policymaking encourage consensus among participants[21]. Unfortunately, though, even when some public servants made conscious efforts to create participation; they commonly made the same mistakes inviting only elite stakeholders[22].

In these deliberative mechanisms, participants exchange ideas, perspectives, experiences, and hence more likely to discover common grounds and interests[23]. With citizens taking positions and exchanging reasons, the deliberative concept has assumed potency and relevance to modern day public administration[24]. This is because the tendency is for participants to aim toward agreements with one another based on reasons, arguments, and principles thereby fostering a consensus in the policymaking process[25]. Although citizens may not have the time and interest to deliberate for the purpose of developing informed public judgments; citizenship participation still remains the cornerstone of democracy[26].

The deliberative concept of policy making is potent and relevant to the modern day public administration. The characteristic exchange of ideas and reasoning make deliberative democracy seems quite ideal[27]. Obvious assumptions are that citizen deliberation can strengthen, not only representative democracy but also create a more informed electorate that would have better holds on the accountability of the political elites and also the processes of policymaking and implementation[28]. Like collaboration, deliberation is seen as a remedy to an uninformed and uninterested public and both should been seen as means of appreciating and recognizing the effects of the public decision-making process[29].

Moreover, insisting that public participation exceeds the bounds of the citizens simply as traditional voters is an important aspect of modern policy administration[30]. Under deliberative public participation, the citizens help to develop and propagate policy through direct and common deliberation mechanisms that would overlap with what currently prevails[31].

The criticism, which is, that citizen-groups will not usually find the time or the expertise for public deliberation is, however, worthy of some consideration[32]. The analysis may be as elusive as attempts to determine what makes the individual interested in public affairs. Deliberation as a policymaking process, therefore, remains likely difficult to create and run. The answer may rest with the call for mandatory attendance of public deliberation in line with summons of jury duties in which attendees would receive travel stipends and reasonable expenses[33].

Public policy as a collaborative process
The collaborative process demands that participants work together to address their public problems, which, they individually cannot address to satisfactory levels[34]. A growing trend exists toward inter-agency collaboration among traditional public agencies. Some public agencies and institutions, recognizing that they cannot solve problems alone, do collaborate on solutions[35]. This collaboration helps solve the most intractable of problems. The new concepts portray that policymaking is not only about proffering solutions but also about creating the processes for collaboration and collective actions[36]. Collaborative governance practices, therefore, increase the capacity of communities to work together to solve common problems.

By providing the avenues for deliberation and subsequent decision-making, the collaborative model serves as a means of giving citizens the knowledge and techniques for dealing with public issues[37]. Collaboration is somewhat ahead of responsiveness in the evolutionary path of government-citizen relationships[38]. This is because collaboration creates the quest for responsiveness that leads to more collaboration and then more responsiveness[39].

Unfortunately, some public officers are still restrained in embracing this concept of collaboration. The reason could be that collaborations are likely to conflict with the parochial political and bureaucratic styles that still define much of the traditional public policy practices. Since collaborative governance practices can resolve intractable public policy problems, producing successful policy outcomes, public administrators should not have any difficulty embracing collaboration[40].

Chapter 6

The Politics of Public Policymaking

The most effective perspective of public policy making in democratic systems is as important as the political system itself. The debates on the aspects of public administration that are relevant to democracy have experiences contrasting and contending, shared views, and very many gray areas. Democracy can, therefore, be viewed and defined through wide and varied angles, each with its ramifications for the policymaking process. By analyzing these perspectives, the practice of democracy and its effects on the policymaking becomes more appreciated.

Public policy is probably the most important aspect of modern life because every aspect of human endeavor is guided by one public policy of the other. The effects of the revolutions in science, education and technology, which have transformed lives from the simple lives of the past to today's complex lives, have made changes in public policy orientation inevitable.

Ideally, no political party would openly advocate public policies that would openly benefit some group at the expense of other groups. The is because, the professed desires in political posturing have always been the enthronement of common good or the protection common of group rights. The reality is that, under the competitive approach to democracy, political have always sought the advancement of group interests, which in most cases have been to the detriment of common good or those of others.

The political process
Politics is the art of balancing interest to resolve conflicts between interests to arrive at a common course of action[1]. The function of the political process should be to galvanize and organize both the individual and private group efforts; to achieve collective goals and objectives that they would ordinarily find difficult, if not impossible, to achieve themselves[2]. Here, the purpose and tendency would be to enthrone common interest rather than self-interest. Hence, the usual outcome of the political process tends to hinge on the principle that no one obtains everything he or she wants; yet everyone obtains something to

satisfy him or herself that the objective is worth pursuing, thereby ensuring more and future participation in the process[3].

Generally, the task of the political system would be: (i) to manage any arising conflicts by establishing rules of participation in the system, (ii) arranging the compromises and balancing interests, (iii) legislating such compromises in the form of the public policy measures, and (iv) creating the structure for enforcing such public policies[4]. Although the outcome of the political process is not usually under the control of a single individual or group, the power and influence one has, one's skills at negotiating, and the strength of other contending interests affects the outcome of the political process; thereby, negating the concept equal representation and equal influence[5].

The driving forces of public policies

Governments, especially the central governments, are the major institutional forces operative in the public policy process[6]. Governments lend legitimacy to policies by making them legal obligations that command the loyalty of the citizens and also monopolize the legitimate use of force to enforce public policies[7]. Official policy-makers are those that have the legal authority to engage in the formation of public policy; such as legislators, executives' administrators and judges[8]. There are, however, primary and supplementary policy-makers. The primary policy-makers (such as the Congress) have direct constitutional authority to act; whereas the supplementary policy-makers (such as the administrative agencies operate on the basis of the authority granted by the primary policy-makers[9]. Essentially, public administrators are the officers that run the machinery of the various levels of government. Generally, the role of the public administrator is the management of public affairs[10]. Hence, many policies do not become public policies until they are adopted, implemented, and enforced by some governmental institutions[11].

The political roles of the stakeholders
A group of decision makers in the public policy process who have been most active and influential in arriving at common courses of actions[12]. They are the elected officials and the public administrators. Although the elected officials and public administrators are directly involved in the process, they are few in comparison with the total populations[13]. Governments need not act before public policies are put into effect as exemplified by the economic sanctions against the apartheid regime of South Africa where religious and secular groups brought pressure to bear on companies doing business with the regime by divesting themselves of their stocks[14].

The Roles of Public Administrators

In the United States, the Constitution provides the "basic political and legal structure, the architecture which prescribes the rules by which a government operates[15]. These public administrators influence public policies through multiple processes. They influence policies when they assume the role s of policy entrepreneurs, or "incubators" of ideas. They are also highly involved in the agenda setting and alternative specification processes of policy making. Often, it is the public administrator that elevates an issue from the status of a condition to that of a problem. More so, in collaboration with other interest groups, they join in the elevation of such problems to the level of government agendas. At the federal level, public administrators implement the decisions and policies spelt out by the legislature and the presidency. Knowing that the administrators run the machineries of governments, it is, therefore, acceptable to argue that, although they are not the primary policy makers, the administrators run the constitution[16].

This role of setting of the agenda for a public problem under a democratic dispensation is undermined by the polar interest of contending parties. To contain the interest of these contending parties, the agenda becomes too obtuse, thereby creating some degree of uncertainty over policy goals. The more obtuse the goals and objectives are, the more the possibility of wider acceptance; and hence, the higher the potentials of elevating them to legislative or administrative agenda.

Generally, government officials do judge policy proposals by it political costs and benefits[17]. The considerations that should guide the development of policy alternatives include cost, stability, reliability, and its flexibility. Other considerations should include communicability, merits, compatibility, and adaptability. Considering that decision makers should be able to forecast the effects of the proposed policy action, it would be necessary to determine if the policy proposals are likely to work; and meet the desired objectives. Simply extrapolating what occurred in the past to what is likely to occur in the future; otherwise called the extrapolation method of evaluating alternative policies could do this. The evaluation of some alternatives may also be on the basis of political analysis. The political analysis refers to the acceptability of the alternatives to the political system[18]. The political analysis dimension should pay the required attention to equity. Essentially, governments should emphasize equity, and adopt policies that seem appropriate for balancing the benefits and harms in a reasonable and equitable manner.

Usually, the perceived manner that the political system would likely react to the proposal also form part of the evaluation consideration. One value public administrators should bring to bear on the society is by working to ensure the accessibility of services to the citizenry. The public administrators ensure the responsiveness and accountability of the government to the governed, the transparency of government actions and services, and the accessibility of all to government programs and services. This policy implementation also comes with its own dose of political maneuvering. Although implementation is a major preoccupation of public administrators, there has been much controversy regarding the best ways for delivery the public programs and services[19].

In Nigeria, there is a relationship between the social and economic status (SES) of an individual and one's level of political participation. Those who are the most advantaged are often better placed than others to advance their interests because they tend to have higher incomes or more education.

Chapter 7

Problems of Policymaking in Nigeria's Local Governments

Most governance reform practices in Nigeria have focused on building up and transforming central state institutions and large cities. Essentially, issues and politics of development have always been constructed from the policy perspectives of large cities. Projects are constituted in a highly centralized and static fashion, with little consideration as to how reforms might be realized within the complex and diverse societies that collectively make up the nation. The interest and fortunes of the governance agenda should be in terms policy that have the potentials of creating impacts throughout a country, as well as encompassing a

diversity of localities within a national space[1].
Hence, the top-down governance reform
practiced in Nigeria is contradictory to genuine
grassroots development.

The factors working against public policy
improvement in the local, state and national
governments in Nigeria are legion. However,
those factors to examine here include problems
with data acquisition, bureaucratic inefficiencies,
nature of governance, and lack of feedback
mechanism.

Problems of data acquisition
The general lack of data in Nigeria makes the
policymaking process and implementation rather
difficult. The key questions for the Nigerian
policy analysts have been on what primary
sources of data would be used for public
administration researches. Generally, data
sources could be from existing literature, self-
collected data such as questionnaires,
government publications, and private
information source publications. The sources of
information that do seem to contain rich
materials for policy analysis are the libraries,
federal agencies, and private organizations.
Unfortunately, these rich sources are scarce; and
public analysts mostly depend on self-
administered questionnaires. In "developing
countries, the administrative personnel and
capacity of the state for collecting and analyzing

data are lacking, and this makes it difficult for governments to understand and develop solutions facing their citizens"[2]. The policy-makers and developers in these developing are hampered by lack of data; hence public actions are mostly guided by guesswork rather than data based analysis[3]. This obviously creates issues of validity and reliability as it relates to what constitutes the major criteria for evaluating the quality of the data collected from these sources. The information critical to the policymaking process in Nigeria is usually in short supply, and often unreliable creating a situation in which policymakers use their intuition and experience rather the analytical information.

Bureaucratic Ineffectiveness
Bureaucratic ineffectiveness is a factor that adversely affects public policy formulation and implementation in municipal governance in Nigeria. Generally, it does seem that the accumulation of the mountains of bureaucratic rules only creates paralysis and thus stifles the drive for changes and new policies. Nigeria's bureaucracies have remained inefficient because of their nature and the rules that set them up and needs to be "tamed". Hence, a major issue of poor performance is the so-called red tape and over regulation that do seem to suffocating creativity. Opening up governance through government-citizenship collaboration would

likely enhance creativity and local adaptation of governance. However, it is pertinent to point out that collaboration is likely to encounter some opposition from the political and bureaucratic systems that have long defined the policy making processes of governments and municipal councils.

Nature of governance

The general nature of governance in Nigerian seems to have assumed the posture of electoral authoritarianism incumbent parties manipulate elections through rigging, bribery, corruption, and intimidation; all designed to thwart the electoral will of the electorate and perpetuate themselves in power. The World Development Bank and the International Monetary Fund (IMF) have persistently indicated that authoritarian environment does not offer any avenues for protest or influence over the policymaking process by interest groups[4]. In addition, many African scholars have argued that the "neopatrimonial" nature of governance in African is largely responsible for the poor performance and failure of public agencies of its countries in these modern times. Neopatrimonial governance is a prevailing state of governance that is "characterized by personalized political authority, weak checks on the private appropriation of public resources; and pervasive clientelism"[5]. Hence, entrenched interest groups control the processes of local administration for their own selfish interest. These groups would usually resist citizen participation and the apparent transparency that goes with such.

Lack of Feedback mechanism

The feedback mechanism shapes the contours of policy implementation. Feedback enables the analyst determines whether the problems are producing the desired results and whether the programs should be modified or terminated, and resources shifted to their programs[6]. As the implementation stage proceeds, progress has to be checked against the set goals to determine if the organization is moving toward its objectives; and decision makers gather the information that tells them how well the decision was implemented and if it was effective in achieving its objectives[7]. Decision makers should also synthesize feedback in shaping the contours of implemented public policies. However, there is no apparent adoption of any feedback mechanism in the public administration process at the various levels of governance in Nigeria.

Chapter 8

Public Policymaking under Democratic Governance

Enduring democratic systems are characterized
by meaningful political participation, peaceful
competition, and democratic values[1]. Democracy
is characterized with such connotations as
responsive governance, high levels of
participation, and high levels of competitive
elections[2].

Such democratic concepts as representation,
participation, and deliberation can be applied to
the processes of policymaking. When these
democratic perspectives are applied to the
policymaking process, their outcomes become as
varied as the concepts. The deliberative and
collaborative perspectives to policymaking do
address the problems of today's policymaking

with regard to creating and enhancing citizen participation in governance.

Obviously, it is the participation, consultation, and bargaining characteristics of democracy, which enables policymakers to forge the prerequisite consensus that is needed to undertake policy initiatives and its attendant policy adjustments[3]. Generally, the formation and implementation of public policy support the establishment of peaceful and stable forms of political competition[4]. Obviously, if one examined any political decision carefully (even a very important one); one would discover that only a tiny proportion of the electorate is actively bringing its influence to bear upon the policymaking politicians[5]. Such democracy principles as the equality of the citizenry, the responsiveness and accountability of the government to the governed, the transparency of government actions and services, and the accessibility of all to government programs and services. These are the values that public administrators bring to bear on public policymaking.

Citizens' participation in Public Policymaking
Citizen participation is an essential part of the democratic process[6]. The traditional democratic theory rests on the assumption that all citizens are- or should become- essentially equal in both their concern with public issues and their

competence to make decisions concerning the issues[7]. Citizen participation is the manner in which citizens communicate their needs to the public officers who, in turn, make necessary decisions[8]. In a democracy, however, everyone is not required to participate because there are too many issues in various places affecting people's lives[9].

Evidently, all citizens cannot participate equally in public decisions and exercise relatively equal amounts of influence in the political system[10]. Despite its importance to the policy making processes of government, understanding what actually constitutes citizen participation, as well as its constituent make-up, has been difficult[11]. If these perspectives should hold, citizens cannot thus be regarded as part of the decision-making processes but merely as the communicators of their individual interests, desires, and demands[12].

Citizens' representation in Public Policymaking

The authority of the state is anchored and derivable from the sovereignty of the people and can only be exercised through their consent. In representative democracy, the people do not govern indirectly by choosing individuals who assemble to put collective wills into action; but rather merely select from among a number of competitors, those who will make political decisions[13]. In modern democratic societies, this consent is mediated through their representatives. Representative policymaking has the advantages of protecting citizens from any direct dangers associated with direct involvement[14]. Further, representation protects the society from uninformed public opinion, and also tends to prevent the tyranny of the majority and can serve as a check on corruption[15].

Representative democracy increases the participation of all citizens regardless of gender, ethnic or religious orientation[16]. Democracy, if practiced in its true form, facilitates a smooth transfer of power from unwilling incumbents, and thus helps to encourage leaders to adopt policies that benefit society at large[17]. In addition, representative democracy meets the needs of a complex, postindustrial society that requires technical, political, and administrative expertise to function[18].

Often, those who participate in the policy-making processes are not the representative spokespersons for the needs and desires of those citizens for whom policies and programs have been designed[19]. Hence, the handpicking of interest groups who participate in public policy debates negates the democratic assumption of equal access of all citizens to direct policy making[20]. On a positive side, although direct participation may be impossible from the practical perspective, broad representation from all segments of the society is not[21].

Citizens' deliberation in Public Policymaking
Deliberative democracy calls for political institutions to adopt deliberation procedures that encourage citizens and their representatives to frame their interests in terms of claims that can be evaluated publicly through rational dialogue[22]. This rational consensus that hence, becomes the normative base for debates within the political system enhances the processes of policymaking.

The contentious perspective of this concept is that laws become legitimate only if they are acceptable to all parties that would be affected by them; after the due consideration in which each party has expressed his or her opinions and concerns over the proposed laws[23]. In this process, the focus shifts from interest groups bargaining and compromise toward the principles of conflict-resolution and other processes that facilitate rational agreement[24]. Generally, public decision-making becomes more deliberative to the extent that it affects the result of an equal and open communication process in which participants appeal to reasons that others can accept rather than to force, money, sheer numbers, or status. Essentially, deliberation "excludes all force…except the force of a better argument"[25].

In a deliberative setting in which the decision rule does seem to demand unanimity, a party wanting to advance self-interests has to take into account how the proposals would help advance the interest of others. The deliberative engagements enhance the potentials for the unanimity of public policy making. Moreover, because each party can anticipate the scrutiny of all others, each participant would formulate policy demands in ways that others would deem valid[26]. This would in turn improve the quality of policy formulation.

No matter how well thought out a proposal may be, however, it is always amenable to improvement by other participants whose own particular points of view gives them access to means of assessment[27]. Ultimately, deliberative democracy enhances the principles of public dialogue, oriented toward the engineering of some forms of rational consensus that would be attractive to those interested in reducing civic indifference, and also those that wish to reduce the dangers of factional politics in policymaking.

Chapter 9

Development under Democratic Governance

Reframing Democratic Governance
The concepts of democracy that developed over the years have shifted from the emphasis on the democratic state to the present day emphasis on the democratic society. There exists an obvious evolution from the state-centered democracy to centering democracy among people[1]. There has been a shift in paradigm from the democratic state to the democratic society that involves a move from citizens as simply voters, and consumers to citizens as problem solvers and co-creators of public goods; from public administrators and elected officials as providers of services and solutions to partners, educators,

and organizers of citizen action; and from democracy as elections to democratic society[2].

Such a shift has the potential to address public problems that governments alone cannot solve, and yet cannot be solved without governments; necessitating the need to cultivate a commonwealth of collaboration[3]. The tools and instruments for the new governance could be channeled through networks of public, private, and nonprofit organizations. This new governance also involves people, who are the toolmakers and tool users; and the processes through which they participate in the work of government[4]. These processes would include such governance concepts as deliberative democracy, e-democracy, public conversations, collaborative policy making, and alternative dispute resolution that would permit citizens and stakeholders to participate actively in the work of government. Public administrators need to address these processes in order to help the public sector develop and use informed best practices[5].

The collaboration of public, private, and nonprofit organizations are the new structures of governance, as opposed to hierarchical organizational decision-making[6]. These faces of the new governance are increasingly becoming important to local government administration. The new governance concepts involve not simply the tools, but also practices and processes for people to participate in the work of government[7]. Public administrators, therefore, ought to facilitate greater citizen engagement in carrying the works of the government[8]. Governance is not simply about elected representatives making value, policy, and tool choices that agencies implement, it is also crucially about the processes that public managers, citizens, and stakeholders use in determining what shape policy, its implementation, and its enforcement will take[9].

Development in a Democratic State
Although disagreements exist among scholars as to which regime type creates more economic growth or provides more public and social services, some studies suggested that modern development can only hastened under democratic dispensation. Some scholars argue that regime types do not have much impact when government performances are measured in terms of economic growth[10]. When, however, government performances are measured in terms of public services, democratic regimes have always outperformed authoritarian regimes[11]. This is especially true for poor democracies and countries that face pressures to provide such social services as education, healthcare, and higher standards of living[12].

All said, political development is central to sustained economic and social development; and when the political process is ineffective, it retards economic and social development[13]. Faltering democratic processes could lead violent civil conflicts, military usurpation of power, arbitrary governance that ignores basic human rights and corrupts the rule of law, or an unresponsive government that is unable to address the basic needs of the society[14]. Successful development depends on the existence of a political environment that aligns political incentives with the requirements for economic development[15]. These political incentives can only be canvassed through improvements in the quality of governance that can be improved through improvement in the level of democratic practices. Essentially, the governance quality central to the development prospects of Nigeria could show that through democracy, improvements will be made in such crucial governance areas as economic policy cohesion, public service effectiveness, and limited corruption[16].

Rural Development Model
Development is when a group of human species in a geographical location acquires the capacities to understand natural law that enables them to collectively organize to increase their capacity of production through technological innovations[17]. The assumption always has been that development is inherently beneficial to societies

and should be promoted through the removal of the various obstacles to development. The conventional development theories had their roots in the problems and experiences of Western societies and not equipped to deal with the problems of the unindustrialized societies[18].

The trend toward the western concepts of development involved the exploitation of natural resources through the infusion of human capital, financial capital and technology into less developed countries, to transit to the modernization, industrialization, and urbanization as in the developed countries[19].

Some economic development models have been used by scholars to explain how societies have developed over the times, namely, the Rostovian, Harrod-Domar, and Lewis models. Scholars postulated these models of development economics because other theories of development seemed only applicable to the developed economies[20]. Of these models, however, the Lewis model of development is more appropriate for the analysis of development the earlier development strategies that were adopted for the rural communities in Nigeria.

The basis of the Lewis theory is that a development process could be triggered by the transfer of surplus labor from the traditional agrarian sector to the new modern, industrial sector[21]. This theory indicates that because of unlimited supply of the unskilled labor required for the rural communities, workers are paid subsistence wages[22]. The urbanized, industrial cities on the other hand, offer higher wages, higher marginal productivity, and initial higher demand for more workers. Over time, the growth of the industrial sector absorbs the surplus labor; thereby promoting industrialization and stimulating sustainable development. As the surplus labor is been used, labor becomes scarcer, and workers are paid on the basis of their marginal product[23]. This transition from traditional to modern economic stage would, however, involve changes in attitudes, creation of need for achievement as well as in social and political institutions[24].

Obviously, Lewis was obviously more interested in the transition of developing economies from dualistic to the one sector of modern economic growth[25]. Lewis considered the solution of development problems to be the focusing of efforts toward changing the operational rules of the global economic system[26]. This Lewis model, incorporated with the power of technology, is still relevant in such heavily populated countries as China, India, Bangladesh, Central America and Sub-Saharan Africa[27].

This dual nature of development in Nigeria sector model of development created traditional agrarian rural communities, characterized by low wages, the abundance of labor, and low productivity. Unfortunately, the primary characteristics of such developing countries as Nigeria are their low income per capita that is even abysmally lower in the rural communities. The goal of national economic development in Nigeria should, therefore, be that of closing the gap in income per capita between the rich and poor communities. This is because, unless the inequality inherent in the duality of the traditional versus modern communities become countered through political or institutional means there is the possibility that violence and political instability could derail the processes of development[28].

The Lewis model erroneously presupposes that the traditional and modern societies are two different stages of development, with their difference disappearing as time progressed. Traditional and modern societies are not opposite ends because both can coexist and supplement each other. Instead of seeing tradition as an obstacle to the drive toward modernization, some traditional elements are also capable of exerting positive effects on the drive toward modernization.

Chapter 10

Local Government Administration under Federalism

Under a true federal structure, the Constitution provides the "basic political and legal structure, the architecture which prescribes the rules by which a government operates"[1]. Generally, the role of public administration is the management of public affairs and the public administrators that run the machinery of the various levels of government constitute the civil service. The machineries of government at the state and local levels do seem similar to the federal level in such regard as the separation of powers of the executive, legislative, and judiciary branches.

In such true federalism as the United States, the 10th amendment to the U.S. Constitution, called the bill of rights, holds that the "'powers not delegated to the United States by the Constitution, nor prohibited by it to the states, are reserved for the states respectively, or to the people" [2]. The inference is that whatever duties the federal government cannot perform must be or should be performed by the states and the local governments. In the United States, this is one of the sources of the responsibilities of public administrators at the state and local governments. The state public administrators in the United States also implement the state legislative laws and executive rules, as spelt out in the states' constitution.

From the foregoing, the original concept of true federalism requires a form of government-to- government collaboration in which a national government shares power with such political sub-units as the states or regional governments. The concept calls for collaborative efforts of these federating units in the design and implementation of the solutions to the problems of the society. From the perspective of developmental economics, there is an underlying assumption that federalism is more effective in dealing with societal problems because of its flexibility and ability to intervene or deal with problems at national, state, and local governments. Programs on education, environmental protection, highways, social welfare, and law enforcement are hence, usually shared by these three tiers of government[3]. With this apparent the transfer of power to the lower levels of government, policy choices are made at levels closer to the people[4], through effective collaboration.

In Nigeria, on the other hand, local government administrators derive most of the responsibilities and powers from the charters establishing such local governments. At this level, most of the administrative heads are the public administrators who usually try to balance political pressures with service delivery. Under this dispensation, government-citizen collaborations have been that exception rather than the rule. For whatever reason, it does seem that the indicative characteristics of Nigeria's administrative state placed the bureaucratic public administrator at the center of decision-making and implementation, thereby giving administrators control over the democratic polity. Although this legal framework was originally designed to protect political and administrative processes from an active citizenry; it has created a situation in which professional administrators tend to deem responsiveness to citizens a necessary evil that sometimes inhibits effective performance. This state of affairs calls for new perspectives to public policymaking and implementation that creates new roles for public administrator through the "localization" of democratic principles.

Chapter 11

The New Trends in Local Government Administration

The previous views of some politicians and public administrators were that providing citizen participation amounted to empowering the people at the expense of administrative and political powers. This perspective was quite faulty because encouraging citizen participation and collaboration in the public management process are positive-sum games[1] that should constitute the backbone of public administration. Moreover, with collaboration, citizens can bring their particular knowledge and skills into the delivery and management of public services, thereby, improving the quality and effectiveness of policy implementation[2]. Observations of public policy formulation and the various efforts at community-rebuilding initiatives have shown that successful initiatives have relied on the community's own resources and strengths as the bedrock for designing change initiatives. As responsive signs of care and willingness to work with citizens to address their concerns and find solutions to their problems, it is of immense importance that public officers meet citizens on their own ground [3]. The hallmark of any active and collaborative initiative should be that conscious efforts be made by public officials to cultivate relationships with all stakeholders before public policy decisions are reached.

Even as citizens have several means to influence public decisions that are made on their behalf by bureaucrats and politicians, this influence ability has been available mostly to the citizens who have higher incomes, more education and more expendable free time at their disposal[4]. Those who are the most advantaged are often been better placed than others to advance their interests. Even when some public servants make conscious efforts to create participation, they commonly make the same mistakes, inviting only elite stakeholders, especially interest groups representatives[5]. Considering that the theories of democracy depend on the practice of political equality[6], this socio-economic bias is quite worrisome. If democracy implies that citizens should participate on equal terms, those at the decision-making table should mirror the composition of the population[7], especially as they reflect gender and racial diversity. With this, more emphasizes should be placed the rights of citizens to be engaged in the decision that touch their lives[8]. Although it is quite difficult to create participation for the entire citizenry, a degree of equality in political participation is symbolically important for a legitimate political system[9], and some minimal level of it is necessary to maintain stability in a political community[10].

This concept of collaboration seems to be the growing trend in government, nonprofit, and business organizations. These citizen-state relationship initiatives often involve more active roles for the citizen in choosing and jointly producing services, often leading to more responsive bureaucracies[11]. A responsive bureaucracy would be moving "towards a more deliberative form that is characterized by collaborative management"[12]. Collaboration, therefore, leads to more responsive bureaucracies[13].

These new governance processes promote increased collaboration among government, business, civil society, and citizens; enhance democratic decision-making; and foster decisional legitimacy, consensus, citizen engagement, public dialogue, reasoned debate, higher decision quality, and fairness among an active and informed citizenry[14]. An undeniable perspective is that these new governance processes can help them build partnerships with citizens and stakeholders to do the work of government in a manner that would increase citizen participation as well effective collaboration[15]. This creates an environment in which it could be wholly acceptable that citizens can and must play an important role in public policy and decision-making. This is because citizens should have the right to decide what is important to them and how they can best achieve their objectives for any claim to be made on the existence of genuine democracy[16].

Chapter 12

New Roles for Local Government Administrators

The key elements of democratic practices are the separation of power, independence of the judiciary, institutionalized checks and balances, participation, competition, and regular free and fair elections. The main attributes of the requirement of free and fair elections are participation, competition, and fairness. The concepts of democracy that had developed over the years have, however, shifted from the emphasis on the democratic state to the present day emphasis on the democratic society. There exists an obvious evolution from the state-centered democracy to centering democracy among people[1].

The paradigm shift from the democratic state

to the democratic society, which created the transition of citizens as simply voters and consumers public services to citizens as problem solvers and co-creators of public goods has redefined the roles of public administrators[2]. This involves shifting from public administrators and elected officials as providers of services and solutions to partners, educators, and organizers of citizen action; and from democracy as processes for conduct of elections toward building democratic societies[3]. Such a shift has the potential to address public problems that governments alone cannot solve, and yet not be solved without governments, necessitating the need to cultivate a commonwealth of collaboration[4].

The changing dynamics of modern societies has created new perspectives of responsive and effective roles for public administrators. The previous perception of public administrators as "aloft" promulgators and implementers of public policy are no longer in vogue. These new governance perspectives require that public administrators serve as the means of facilitating public participation and citizen-government collaboration: as team players, as creators of shared responsibilities, as protectors of social equity, and as joint implementers of public policies.

As vehicles for citizen participation

The extent to which the administration of a representative government can accommodate active citizens' involvement in the public decision-making process has always been a key issue in public administration[5]. Public administrators serve as vehicles of citizen participation in varieties of ways. They have the discretionary powers to invite direct citizen participation in developing public policy, or discourage it, or even prevent it in the course of whatever duties they have been assigned to perform[6]. The need to encourage active citizen participation remains important because "democratic tradition depends on the existence of an engaged citizenry, active in all sorts of groups, associations, and governmental units"[7].

Michael Sandel expressed the view of situations in which citizens look beyond their narrow interest to the broader public interest; adopting wider perspective that require knowledge of public affairs; sense of communality showing more concern for the whole rather than the narrow self-interest[8]. Public administrators should, therefore, embrace these new initiatives in which individuals are more actively engaged in governance.

As Facilitators of Government-Community collaboration

The view that public administrators should focus

their responsibilities on serving and empowering citizens as they manage public organizations and implement public policies is obviously incontestable[9]. This contemporary model of governance rests on the perspective that the major reason for the existence of governments is to ensure citizens can make the choices that reflect with their self-interests[10]. The need exists for public administrators to encourage government-community collaboration. Usually, these communities do constitute the platforms that people use to work out their personal interests within the confines of community interests, concerns, and common good. These are also the platforms that citizens use to engage one another in personalized dialogues and deliberation that have become the main thrust of community building and spirits.

The crucial role of the public administrator would be the creation, facilitation, and support of these connections between governments, citizens, and their communities[11]. There has been a transition from the earlier public administration perspective of the citizens as consumers to the recognition of citizens as partners or collaborators with the administrators[12]. By creating arenas in which citizens, through deliberation can articulate mutual interest and values, public servants advance the problem-solving potentials of the concerned communities[13]. Many scholars do agree that, in public policymaking of today, the programs and policies guide the society by giving structure and direction to social and political life are the outcome of a complex set of interactions involving multiple groups, multiple interests, and different opinions[14]. Public servants should, therefore, see citizens as citizens that should share authority and responsibility, rather than as voters or clients are in consonance with this new view and roles for public administrators[15].

As Team players

The primary role of government should not only be the direction of public actions, nor the establishment rules and incentives, but rather as another important player in the process of moving the communities toward the desired goals and visions[16]. The contention that the increasingly important role of the public servant is to help citizens articulate and meet their shared interests, rather than to attempt to control or steer society in new directions seems quite acceptable[17].

As creators of shared responsibilities

The new perspectives in public administration entails that the process of establishing new visions for society should not, in any way, be left to elected or appointed public officials[18]. Rather, it should be the vision of shared responsibilities among the government, the governed, and the major stakeholders. The public administrators should commit to building collective notions of the public interest; with the goal of proffering solutions, and the desire to create common interests and responsibilities.

The role of public officials should be increasingly to create the enabling environments that would, in public settings, provide for unfettered access to arenas that promote unconstrained public deliberation[19]. The outcome of such deliberations would enable the community develop the ideas to solve, not only their immediate problems but also develop the problem solution guidelines for future concerns.

As Protectors of social Equity

As protectors of social equity, government has moral obligations to ensure that the solutions that arise from such deliberative processes not only take full cognizance but also are consistent with the norms of justice, equity, and fairness. Government should not only act as facilitators of the solutions to public problems but should also ensure that both in substance and process, those solutions are aligned with the interest of the public[20]. The role of government should be that of ensuring the predominance of the welfare of the public. To ensure that the society enhances equity in its public policymaking process, the values enshrined in most democratic constitutions, which presumes that all are created equal and should so be treated. In its ideal sense, all citizens should be guaranteed the same rights and services from the government; hence the concept of equity in public affairs. The drive toward equity in public affairs should also lead to the introduction of social welfare programs.

As Joint Implementers

The implementation of the policies and programs tailored to meet public needs can be most effectively achieved through collective and collaborative efforts. The idea is not for the collaborating and deliberating public to develop the vision, leaving the implementation to public servants, but it is rather to ensure that all stakeholders join in the process of carrying out the envisioned programs[21]. This could be done by politically compelling the elected officials to articulate and encourage processes that strengthen the participatory responsibility of the citizenry[22]. This could be achieved by creating openness, accessibility, and responsiveness criteria that are designed to meet the needs of the people.

Chapter 13

The Challenges of Policymaking in Local Government Administration

A new trend toward inter-agency collaboration among traditional public agencies has evolved. This is so because public agencies have found that they must collaborate with others to find solutions to these shared problems[1]. Such issues as environmental pollution, terrorism, and transportation that transcend jurisdictional boundaries have, hence, found solutions in inter-governmental and multi-sectorial collaboration[2]. Multi-sector Collaboration is one of the ways to accomplish common goals involving public, community, and even nonprofit organizations toward solving the common problems affecting a community.

Managing Shared Problems

The management of these shared problems requires unique and new strategies that revolve around mutual benefits. These needs for managing shared problems also call for partnership the three sectors of government, private, and nonprofit sectors. Public administrators in state and local entities should work together in ways that seek to provide services of quality at least cost because of these commonalities that exist between public and private and nonprofit entities[3]. These partnerships are becoming more common probably because collaboration promises greater service satisfaction, increased flexibility for change, problem solving, and innovation, and cost saving measures[4]. To achieve this, the public administrator would have to encourage strategic collaboration and alliances between business, government and the nonprofit organizations based on what is common among them. This collaboration is propelled by political, economic and social forces as well as the need for governments to deliver cheaper and more efficient services to the citizens.

The Increasing Cultural Diversity of the Society

The values championed by a society are a product of complex historical processes that involve social, economic, and political lives of the citizens[5]. The values become more complex and diverse as the cultural diversity of the society increases. This is because each culture has its own norms, values, and unique concepts of social issues. It will, therefore, be ethnocentric for any individual to believe that his or her values and ethics are perfect and normal way[6] especially with regard to policy making in societies with diverse cultures and values.

Although public administrators have values based on religious beliefs, family background, heritage, or ethnicity, they must interpret these values and act in a way that is reasonably and objectively ethical, and based on their field of practice, regardless of any cultural influence. Notwithstanding that the role of the public administrator is to objectify values and ethics regardless of any cultural viewpoints[7], the administrator must take the cultural diversity of a society into cognizance. They not only need to be culturally sensitive, but also need to balance that with the basic objective of discerning right from wrong, or good from evil.

Issues of Social equity in Policymaking

Fairness in the delivery of public services hinges

on the principle that each citizen regardless of economic resources or personal traits has the right to receive equal treatment by the political system. H. George Frederickson, one of the most prominent equity scholars referred to social equity as the "third" pillar of public administration[8]. Social equity is construable as the fair and just treatment as well as the equal and equitable distribution of benefits to the society at large[9]. Frederickson argued that considering that the procedures of representative democracy operate in ways that do not adequately reverse systematic discrimination against minorities, social equity would include the activities designed to enhance the political power and economic wellbeing of these minorities[10]. Hence, the contention that the two pillars of public administration; namely efficiency and effectiveness, are contingent on the strength of the third pillar, which is, social equity remains valid[11].

The Ethical Challenges

Ethics could be viewed as a system of moral principles; and thus the moral compass that guide us in our decisions. Ethics are about right and wrong, good and bad, benefit and harm, and they define the nature of public managers and administrators[12]. Ethics, simply put, are "how our actions affect other people, of peoples' right and duties, and of the rules people apply in making decision"[13]. The standards of conduct that indicate how one should behave based on moral duties and virtues reflect the ethics of a given society.

Usually, issues of ethics tend to exist in virtually most public decision-making processes. Ethical dilemmas, therefore, arise when right or wrong cannot be clearly identified, and each alternative has a potentially harmful ethical consequence. Unfortunately, there seems to be some measure of acceptance that some collective actions, carried out through government almost never benefit some people without in some sense, harming others. The utilitarian perspective of "public good for the greatest number" is, hence, the more often adopted criterion in designing solutions to public problems, and the resolution of public ethical issues.

This utilitarian perspective essentially supports that though a public policy action may be harmful to certain groups, the act is right if it produces the greatest good for the greatest number of people affected by the action[16.] To reduce the incidence of harm or analyze the appropriateness of a public policy decision, the public administrator could employ the normative concept of "ethical triangle", created by the analysis of the mutual dependence of cognitive and virtue ethics. The essence of this ethic triangle is that it creates the guide that the best ethical perspective would have to pass the issues of concern through the ethical crucibles of all the three apexes of this equilateral triangle. The apexes of this equilateral triangle are justice, greatest good and integrity[14].

The justice apex demands that rights be exercised in a way that is fair to all. The strength of this apex is that it requires that individuals or situations that are similar in the aspects found relevant to a decision be treated the same way. For instance, men and women should receive equal pay for the same job. The integrity apex is of the essence because the only real credibility of a public administrator has is his or her integrity[15].

This apex indicates that an act is right if it produces the greatest good for the greatest number of people affected by the action. The apex that holds that moral behavior should produce the greatest good for the greatest number seems to be the utilitarian and has the weakness of the possibility that it may be it may be harmful to some others. The ethical challenge becomes to reduce or protect others from the harmful effects.

Although the key criteria that should guide the policy analyst in identifying policy problems is if it affects a substantial number of people with broad effects[17], the solutions must be balanced by their possible benefits and harm to others. The issues of ethics should be those of social responsibility and the administrator must determine its responsibility to the political system; deciding how to balance and reconcile that with its responsibility to the nation, the society, and humanity at large.

Chapter 14

Improving the Policy Process in Local Governance

Although there is a disconnection between theory and practice of democracy in the so-called democratic institutions, it is pertinent to indicate that sound decision-making can still occur without the participation of all and sundry in the society. The crucial dimensions to policy formulation and implementation are the collaboration between public administrators and the citizenry.

Although there is still a measure of ambivalence among citizens and administrators on the value of direct participation, ample evidence exists of the benefits of collaboration. When done correctly, participatory and collaborative governance produce positive outcomes. The challenge to public administrators is to find the right balance between responsive, and efficient administration, and people-centered deliberative and collaborative decision making.

Public administrators ought to facilitate greater citizen engagement because governance is also about the processes that public administrators, citizens, and stakeholders use in determining what shape a policy, its implementation, and its enforcement will take. The alternative and nongovernmental vehicles for influencing the public policymaking processes such as nonprofit organizations, professional associations, interest groups, think tanks and political action committee have become more relevant. These new governance tools involve the citizens and processes through which the citizens participate in the work of governance. These processes would include such governance processes as deliberative democracy, e-democracy, public conversations, collaborative policymaking, and alternative dispute resolution, to permit citizens and stakeholders to participate actively in the work of government.

Nonprofit Organizations
Nonprofit organizations constitute social capital asset and agents and thereby contribute immensely to the public policy process[1]. The nonprofit organizations regulate, facilitate, assist,

and modify markets as well as playing significant roles in every aspect of public policy, stretching from the determination of party platforms to the implementation of policies[2]. The tools and instruments for the new governance are channeled through the networking of nonprofit organizations with public and private institutions. These collaborations are the new structures of governance, designed to make public administration more effective, as opposed to hierarchical organizational decision-making[3]. These faces of the new governance are becoming increasingly important to the operation of international, national, state, and local public institutions.

Professional Associations
The schools of thought that propound representation as the key aspects of democracy argue that the central contributions of associations consist of enhancing the quality of representation and public deliberation[4]. German sociologist and philosopher, Jurgen Habermas had argued that the chief contribution of associations is to facilitate public deliberation through the generation and dissemination of convictions[4]. Proponents of direct citizen participation in democracy emphasize that associations bring forth face-to-face cooperation in the pursuit of collective ends[5]. The most cogent contributions of associations to

democracy are, therefore, on their potentiality to reinvigorate massive democratic participation[6].

From these dual perspectives, the participatory democrats consider the most important contribution of associations as either direct participation in public governance or political resistance[7]. Essentially, the contributions of associations rest on their ability to create and facilitate representation and deliberation[8]. In democratic societies, however, the most important contributions of associations are dependent on the distinctive features of the political context of the society[9]. Where the levels of economic and human development are low, the most important contributions of associations become the organization and mobilization of individuals to help contribute to the provision of public goods or to ensure that scarce resources are equitably distributed[10]. This is because; the advancement of one's purpose is a central component of individual freedom, democratic states, and institutions.

In addition, the basic notion that organized associations can act as a source of countervailing power against state authority has made resistance to domination and antidemocratic power to be a central contribution of associations to democratic governances[11]. When properly organized, associations can offer resistance to tyrants, authoritarians, or antidemocratic forces. For instance, student, worker, civic, and professional associations have contributed to democratic reform processes by restraining and holding public servants and political office holders accountable to the law and public expectations of responsible governance[12]. Jurgen Habermas indicated that though these associations cannot solve the problems they raise, they can, however, set the public agenda and also steer formal political systems in the directions created by fair deliberation[13]. The interest groups, public interest organizations, and social-movement organizations contribute to public deliberation by seeking to address and persuade the broader public[14]. Representative government improves when associations foster the disposition of individuals toward participation in civic life and teaching the necessary political skills[15].

Political/Social Interest Groups

Interest groups such as political action committees, political groups and environmental protection groups and consumer protection groups constitute potent vehicles of influencing policymaking in a democratic dispensation. Interest groups are a crucial line between citizens and governments[16]. A public interest group is one that seeks a collective good, the achievement of which will not selectively and materially benefit the member of the organization and hence, not self-serving[17]. Accepting that there is a relationship between membership in an organization and participation in politics means that citizens' groups have the potential of mobilizing relatively large numbers of individuals[18]. By so doing, interest groups increase the potentials for mass participation in the policymaking process.

Localized Governance: Neighborhood Councils/Town Unions

Strengthening neighborhood councils or town development unions could be another way of advancing the policy making process in Nigeria's local governments. These town associations and neighborhood council's models are examples of citizen participation strategy that have emerged newly in the field of democratic governance and public administration. Citizen participation in local governance and agencies would provide a valuable process that initiates meaningful interaction and dialogue among citizens and public administrators leading to an improved understanding of service delivery[19]. This concept of this localized governance entails the empowerment of the people through collaboration, using their neighborhood councils or town unions.

Although the argument among scholars has been on the designs and processes of citizen participation that would best serve given situations, neighborhood councils are probably the best suited to bring the government processes closest to the citizens[20]. The primary opinion on which services local governments should render to citizens is better served, more realistic, and more realizable through the process of encouraging and creating neighborhood councils[21]. Although there could be administrative mandates requiring public administrators to provide for citizen participation, these are typically done out of political expediency and have been ineffective because they were top-down approaches[22]. These approaches have even been made worse by the minimalist approached adopted by public administrators to the implementation of the mandates[23].

In contrast, neighborhood councils would allow citizens to create grass-root approaches that would enhance the quality and effectiveness of governance at local levels[24]. Another benefit of strengthening neighbor councils would be that of using the apparent engagement of the citizens to sustain such democratic principles[25] as deliberation, participation, and citizen-government collaboration. Citizen organizations such as neighborhood councils and town development unions constitute an appropriate vehicle for citizen participation in governance especially at the local government level by serving as incubators of new ideas and as a feedback mechanism to the public policy implementation process[26].

Chapter 15

Development Unions/Neighbourhood Associations as Development Partners

Other than the governments, the alternative ways that could be adopted to solve societal problems do seem to be the involvement of the nonprofit organizations and collaboration between the nonprofit and the private sector. Local citizen organizations such as neighborhood associations and town union are recommendable strategies to allow citizens to create grass-root structures within the framework of the processes of governance. Since modern day governance requires that public policies are set to satisfy societal values, involving local neighbourhood associations in active public participation and engagement is quite important[1]. Citizen organizations such as neighbourhood councils and town unions have become very imperative as the most appropriate means for citizen participation at the local level of governance. In conjunction with public institutions, it is recommendable these associations should also play greater roles in policy formulation, coordination, and enforcement[2].

The mechanisms through which democratic principles advance policymaking process can be better understood by delving into the relationship between associations and democracy. The involvement of grass root associations reinforces representative democracy, therefore enhancing democracy. Whereas the representative perspective to democracy posit that associations enhance the quality of representation and public deliberation, the participatory dimension of democracy emphasize that those associations contribute to direct participation.

The need for this 'localization' of democracy derives from the rationales of national and local politics. Experiences have shown that the local appropriation of democracy creates legitimacy for local political leaders, who will in turn mobilized local resources for development[3]. When localized, democracy leads to an increased degree of local resource mobilization or at least an increased awareness among the local political elite of its necessity[4].

There is an intrinsic link between popular participation at the local level, better government at the local level, and the mobilization potential for local development[5]. The introduction of democracy at local level sometimes unleashes transformative forces with potentials for positive and far-reaching long-term effects[6]. This is because today's social and economic development depends on the existence of a political environment that brings political incentives and the requirements for economic development into consonance[7]. The level of economic and human development of the society would, however, influence the roles the associations would assume for themselves[8].

Added to the fact that, with citizen participation, policies become more in tune with the preferences of the citizens; and citizens also become more likely to become supportive evaluators of the government policymaking and implementation processes[9]. The role of government becomes that of bringing the stakeholders together as collaborator bent on designing solutions to public problems[10]. This citizenship participation creates a healthy democratic system because the engagement of the citizenry is much better than passiveness[11]. Administrators should, therefore, engage citizens with one another so that they come to develop mutual understanding, goals and interest[12].

This collaboration occurs when people and organizations combine to produce something through joint efforts, resources, and decision-making and share ownership of the product or service[13]. Usually, collaborative relationships hinge on shared knowledge and decision-making; and obviously assume that citizens are capable of governing themselves by providing citizens with open and non-threatening forums for deliberation and decision-making[14]. The process becomes collaborative when it is inclusive of all interests and concerns relevant to the policy issues[15]. This is in contrast with the traditional top-down model of the state-citizen relationship in which citizens simply cast their votes for the elected officials who control and direct the bureaucracies[16]. The traditional model is even on the decline in most Western democracies, as the demand for collaboration increases.

Generally, encouraging citizen participation in the public management process is a positive-sum game and that with collaboration; citizens can bring their particular knowledge and skills into the delivery and management of public services[17]. This is especially important as collaborative governance practices can enhance the capacity of individuals, communities, and organizations in the quest to solve the collective problems of the society[18].

Chapter 16

Strategic Planning in Local Government Administration

Most developing countries are constantly and continuously confronted with the issues of infrastructural development to the extent that the standard of living of the citizenry is under constant threat. The situation has a tremendous degradation effects on the standards of living of these countries. While it is the job of governments to look out for the interest and wellbeing of its citizens, it is the appointed interest of every shareholder to contribute as much as possible. The developing countries, however, need their local and national governments to take more responsibility to obtain needed cooperation and build infrastructure.

Although developing the infrastructures for better living conditions in any country is the primary responsibility of the political leadership, there is the need for government-citizen collaboration. Unfortunately, there has been lack of collaboration between the various stakeholders from the three sectors of business, nonprofit and local governments in Nigeria. Overcoming the barriers facing each of the three sectors in meeting the objective of improving the standard of living of the people would require the building of a collaborative network of these key stakeholders. To create a sustainable and successful partnership, the government, private, and nonprofit sectors must ensure that there is involvement and investment at all levels.

Fortunately enough, partnerships between non-profit, business and government sectors are becoming more pronounced in most countries as the societal problems become more complex and difficult for the individual sectors while practitioners increasingly realize the benefits of collaboration. The challenges facing the administrators are to determine clear and strategic direction of their development projects, whether the council's resources and competences can accomplish the chosen strategy, and what could be done to sustain or improve the implementation of the project. The stages of strategic planning involve in the development of these projects are, action plans, implementation, monitoring, and evaluation.

Action Plans
An action plan is a series of steps that were crucial to particular units of work[1]. An action plan is a "highly effective management tool for establishing a program/project, ensuring that it is clearly and properly designed". Action plans focus on work to be completed, resource to complete the work, duration of the work, monetary cost of the work and source of money to be expended. The purpose of the plan is to craft and elucidate on the design of a program/project, produce review and approval process and make available, yardsticks for evaluating program progress.

The general components of an action plan include the definition of purpose, which provides the rationale behind the program; showing problem definition and how to positively address the problem; calculation of the necessary inputs to achieved needed objectives in terms of cost of financial, human and material resources, and the definition and extent of outputs in terms of projected results from the expended inputs.

Developing an action plan starts with stating the objective and goals[2]. The defining objective of the program/project ensures that short-term and long-term outcomes realized. If the program/project is not meeting these goals, adjustments could be made to align current results with desired outcomes. To meet the desired objectives, an action plan must outline the strategic direction the project as to create and elevate the implementation processes to a higher level of certainty.

Implementation
The principal preoccupation of public administrators is project implementation[3]. The value public administrators bring to bear on the society is by working to ensure the accessibility of services to the citizenry through the implementation process. The implementation plan takes the strategic process to the level of the individual and also forms the basis of personnel assignment and performance measures[4].

The critical factors that are necessary for a successful plan implementation are the development and adoption of the strategies and goals that conform to the objectives, and being able to communicate them to the workers. The implementation process essentially involves the putting the short-term objectives into action; first, by communicating the plans and strategies to the employees and by allocating resources to the processes. When then implementation processes are in operations, the processes are then continuously monitored and evaluated.

The implementation process also needs control. The implementation control would assess whether or not the planned course should be changed with regards to the elements or issues that have come to light during implementation. The implementation control is not designed to ensure that implementation goes on as planned, but rather as a monitoring tool for specific phases or elements of the strategy as they relate to performance management plan.

Monitoring and Performance Evaluation
A well-developed Performance Measurement System will enable its users to spot weaknesses and threats, as well as strengths and opportunities[5]. Monitoring provides the user with the results needed to decide whether or not the targets are met or not"[6]. In this evaluation stage, "decision makers gather information that tells them how well the decision was implemented and whether it was effective in achieving its objectives"[7].

Performance measurement contributes to better decision making, performance appraisal, accountability, service delivery, public participation and improvement of civic communication[8]. Performance measurement is an essential tool for addressing issues of productivity improvement; especially, from the perspectives of efficiency, effectiveness, and accountability"[9].

The six crucial criteria against which the performance of programs can be measured are;

the delivery of quality service, productive use of resources, citizen satisfaction, deriving adequate resources, administrative rationality and catering to important interests and stakeholders[10]. Performance measurement is important because it allows the public administrator evaluate how well the resources are meeting the goals and objectives that have been set in the action plan; as well as the assessment of the effectiveness of the plan by stakeholders[12]. Performance measurements also enable public administrators to evaluate the performance of individuals and agencies tasked with accomplishing the tactics and objectives of the strategic plan[13].

The policies and programs that are decided upon and carried out must always keep the strategic outcomes and intent in mind, while also providing for performance management measures that can determine real progress and value for the money expended on them. Making the plan clear and concise and communicating the same creates the basis for transparency as well as feedback and the means to make what are the inevitable midcourse corrections.

Chapter 17

Example of Governance by Collaboration:

Waste Management Strategies for Local Governments

The Project Concept

Effective policymaking has some definite ties to democratic principles and the application of the democratic principles of collaboration and citizen participation should be the bedrock for creating the enabling environment that gives renewed vigor to the public policies designed to improve the sanitary condition within a metropolitan council.

Overcoming the barriers facing the Nigerian local governments in meeting the objective of waste management would, therefore, require the building of a collaborative network of the key stakeholders. Although the government can, in concert with private and nonprofit groups and organizations, seek solutions to the problems that communities face, collaborating with the citizenry engineers more encompassing benefits, both economically, and politically. The need exists for the government to brace up to the occasion by encouraging more collaboration and allocating more resources to the environmental sanitation sector.

The local governments in Nigeria have sub-units called wards. Each of these wards would constitute a neighborhood council in the urban areas. The driving forces to emphasize would be the need to work collaboratively through project teams, deepening professional skill base, through training programs; regularly assessing the purposes and goals, through monitoring and evaluation; and gaining entirely new skills through the training programs and citizen-government collaboration.

Problem Analysis

The barriers that militate against the realization of the objective of improving the environmental sanitation of the urban local governments in Nigeria are the lack of appropriate waste disposal facilities, lack of the necessary infrastructure for mass education, and the lack of collaboration between the municipal council and its residents. Others include the lack of skilled and professionally trained health workers and the negative attitudes of the residents toward environmental sanitation. Another problem of environmental sanitation chiefly arises from the open drainage systems, not usually maintained the local authorities or the residents.

The low morale of current employees and the unavailability of well-trained workforce could also constitute barriers to effective collaboration. The opportunities to realize from these situations are public health education, skill development and training, and the provision of waste management facilities.

Opportunity analysis
Although the problem of waste management continues to defy the efforts of the local and state governments in Nigeria, beneficial opportunities could arise from the expected collaborations. The expected benefits include enhanced business opportunities and improvement in the health status of the residents. The collaborative networking would present opportunities for skill development and training, the development of environmental health programs, and the provision of the appropriate facilities for garbage disposal. Other opportunities include the education of the residents on the need for

enhanced environmental sanitation, and the relationship between decent health and appropriate sanitation. A potential opportunity is that these neighborhood councils could eventually be the cornerstones for neighborhood policing and law enforcement. There would also be an opportunity to create a new set of values that would most likely strengthen and extend the visions, values and missions of the major stakeholders of the council. The collaboration will also offer an opportunity to develop effective plans for communication with the citizens, thereby enhancing further citizen participation in the entire democratic process.

Action Plan

The critical factors for a successful plan implementation are the development and adoption of the strategies and goals that conform to the objectives, and being able to communicate them to the other collaborators. Preparation and planning also create and elevate the implementation processes to a higher level of certainty.

Objectives

Prior definition of project objectives ensures that short-term and long-term outcomes are realized. The desired short-term outcomes are: improving the environmental sanitation of the local government area, creating a sustainable health management program for the city and creating a good business environment for the residents. If, however, the program is not meeting these goals, then the program manager should make adjustments that align current results with desired outcomes.

The participating neighborhood associations would need to create the ability to develop action plans, as well as creating new ideas and concepts. This requires the reinforcement of the favourable perspectives, overcoming obstacles, and ignoring negative tendencies. The essence is to develop the strategies that would be sustainable and enduring enough for the unforeseen future.

Goals

First, there is a need to develop set goals and values. If there are no pre-conditions (set goals) that could guide collaborative actions to agreeable solutions, the individuals tend to act from their own perspectives. At any moment in time, it is those set of goals that would define the purposes and mission of the project. The attainment of these goals would define the success or failure of the project. The goals of the project could, for instance, be; to provide garbage disposal bin at every major street junction, to deploy one sanitation inspector per every 200 residential buildings, to provide garbage collection trucks, and to embark on massive health education street health campaigns.

Strategies
For any project be successful, the collaborators are required to have the resources and competences to carry out the chosen strategies. The strategy should also be predicted upon the internal resources and capabilities of the collaborating entities. The aim will be to determine whether the existing strategies and infrastructures are satisfactory and adequate, and whether the proposed strategies will be satisfactory. In most Nigerian local governments, the existing strategies and infrastructures are unsatisfactory and inadequate, which is why they experience many environmental issues and problems. These problems include the lack of appropriate waste disposal facilities, the absence of the necessary infrastructures for the mass education of the residents on the issues of sanitation, lack of skillful and professionally trained sanitation inspectors, and the negative attitudes of the residents toward environmental sanitation.

Need Assessment
For effective government-citizen collaboration in these kinds of projects, the conduct of a need

analysis is always necessary. The collaborating partners would work out the total manpower and resource needs of the project and such should fall within the recourses and capabilities of the partners. The respective responsibilities and roles of the parties involved in the project needs must be defined. The local government could, for instance, provide the needed manpower (sanitation inspectors) that would monitor and enforce compliance to set health standards, sanctioning, and possibly prosecuting violators. The local governments could also provide the garbage bins and garbage trucks needed by each ward. The neighborhood councils would provide the volunteers needed for effective health education campaigns and public enlightenment and could also bring aboard, new ideas that would enhance the process of health education.

Generating the revenue needed to meet the stated goals and objectives requires that the processes that would be effective in determining the resource capacities, capabilities, and limitations of the partners must be adopted. The slow pace of government actions creates an environment in which these local governments customarily have less capacity for revenue mobilization. A joint team of local government and neighborhood associations' officials could be responsible for collecting the stipulated monthly payment for the program; and for creating, and sustaining public health enlightenment campaigns. Some other collaborative teams would be needed to separately implement, monitor, and evaluate the project.

Project Implementation
The implementation process essentially involves putting the short-term objectives into action by communicating the plans and strategies to the residents of the council and allocating resources to the processes. The success of this project depends on the translation of the strategies into action. Sometimes this never happens especially when the implementing entities lack the resources and energy required to translate the objectives into action. Essentially, the strategies must be translated into the appropriate tactical plans, programs, and budgets.

Generally, the recommended implementation strategies are:

1. Identify the leading deliverables.
2. Gear plans toward major deliverables rather than toward time,
3. Expend money step-by-step rather than up-front.
4. Set a monitoring system.

The steps that could constitute the roadmaps to the implementation process are:

1. To create the major deliverables such as the number garbage bins expected to be in place at the specific time frames.

2. Focus project plans by tying expenditure to number of installed garbage bins and the number of health enlightenment literature distributed.

3. Creating monitoring and feedback systems.

4. Creating joint teams would be responsible for creating and carrying the responsibilities defined by the deliverables. See appendix 1 for the implementation plan.

Project Monitoring and Performance Evaluation

When the implementation processes are in operations, the processes should be monitored and evaluated continuously. As the implementation stage proceeds, progress should be checked against the deliverables and timeline to determine if the project is moving toward its objectives. The monitoring team would be responsible for this process.

At intervaled stages, the evaluation team gathers the information that indicates how well the decisions are been implemented and whether they were effective in achieving desired objectives. The adopted metrics for evaluation would be, the number of garbage bins in place, the number of trucks deployed, the number of households with improved sanitary conditions, and the cleanliness of the local government area. This will be enhanced by regularly assessing purpose and goals. Evaluating the results of a project is a key to continuing the efforts that have begun. It is important to note that success often depends on all participants being accountable for active participation. The collaborating partners must have similar expectation about the program, have confidence that each partner will follow through, and be able to measure the outcomes. See appendix 2 for the evaluation metrics.

APPENDIX 1: The Implementation Plan

Deliverable	Timeline	Who is Responsible
Statutory creation of the neighborhood/resident associations	Two months	The local government council
Election of association officers	Two months	The Ward Residents
Develop strategies and strategic plans for waste management	One month	The Implementation Team
Provision and distribution of public health enlightenment literature	One month	The local government Council/The Ward Associations
Provision of garbage bins	Two months	The local government council
Deployment of garbage trucks	One month	The local government Council
Monitoring the Implementation	Continuous	The Monitoring Team
Evaluation of the process	Every Three months	The Evaluation Team
Progress Report	Bi-annual	All Partners/Collaborators

Appendix 2: The Evaluation Metrics

End-State Goals	Metrics	Target
To provide garbage disposal bin at every major street junction	The number of garbage bins in place	80 garbage bins
Deploy one sanitation inspector per every 200 households	The number of deployed sanitation Inspectors	Five Sanitation Inspectors
To provide four garbage collection trucks.	The number of garbage collection trucks deployed	Four garbage collection trucks
Embarking on massive health education street health campaigns	The number of public health information literature distributed	Given to every household
Changing the attitudes of the residents toward environmental sanitation.	Percentage of positive sanitation reports	Better health habits of residents
Creating a sustainable health management program	Positive reports from all stakeholders	Continuous
Creating a sustainable and successful government-citizen partnership	Continuous citizen-government collaboration	Continuous
Opportunity for other uses	Adoption of Collaborative process to other local problems	Continuous

ENDNOTES

CHAPTER 1

[1]Manin, B. 1997. *The Principles of Representative Government.*Uk: Cambridge University Press.

[2]Tocqueville, A. 1930. In Shafritz, J.M; Hyde, A.C. & Parkes, S.J. 2004. *Classics of Public Administration.*5th Ed. Belmont (CA): Wadsworth/Thompson Learning.

[3]Freeman, S. 2000. Deliberative Democracy: A Sympathetic Comment. *Philosophy and Public Affairs.* *29* (4), p.371.

[4]Matheson, C. 1987. Weber and the Classification of Forms of Legitimacy. *British Journal of Sociology, 38*(2). 199-215.

[5]USAID Policy. 1991. *Democracy and Governance.* Washington, DC

[6]Dahl, R.A. 1956. *A Preface to Democratic Theory.* Chicago: The University of Chicago Press.

[7]Lipstz, K.L. 2004. *Campaigns and Competition: How to Enhance Voter Knowledge and Deliberation in Mass Democracy.* Ph. D. Dissertation. University of California. Berkley, United States.

[8]Schumpeter, J. A. 1947. *Capitalism, Socialism and Democracy.* London: George Allen and Unwin.

[9]Ibid.

[10]Cain, B. E. 1999. In Lipstz, K.L. 2004. *Campaigns and Competition: How to Enhance Voter Knowledge and Deliberation in Mass Democracy.* Ph.D. Dissertation, University of California, Berkley, United States.

[11]Ibid.

[12]Schumpeter, J.A. 1942. In Harris, S.E. 1951. *Schumpeter: Social Scientist.* Boston, MA: Harvard University Press.

[13]Freeman, Samuel. 2000. Deliberative Democracy: A Sympathetic Comment. *Philosophy and Public Affair, 29* (4), p.371.

[14]Harris, S.E. 195. *Schumpeter: Social Scientist* .MA; Harvard University Press.

[15]Lipstz, K.L. 2004. *Campaigns and Competition: How to Enhance Voter Knowledge and   Deliberation in Mass Democracy.* Ph.D. Dissertation, University of California, Berkley, United States.

[16]Ibid.

[17]Cremona, R.K. 2006. *A Meaningful Majority: Rediscovering Government by the People.* Ph.D. Dissertation, State University of New York New York, United States.

[18]Dahl, R.A. 1989. *Democracy and its Critics.* Connecticut: Yale University Press.

[19]Riker, W.H.1993. Comments on Radcliff's "liberalism, populism and Collective Choice". *Political Research Quarterly, 46* (1). 143-149.

[20]Dahl, R.A. 1963. *Who Governs? Democracy and Power in the American City.* New Haven, CT: Yale University Press.

[21]Campbell, Heather and Robert Marshall. 2000. Public Involvement and planning: Looking beyond the One to Many. *International planning Studies, 5*(3), 321-344.

[22]Freeman, S. 2000. Deliberative Democracy: A Sympathetic Comment. *Philosophy and Public Affairs, 29* (4), p.371.

[23]Bohman, J., and W. Rehg. 1997. *Deliberative Democracy: Essays on Reason and Politics.* Harvard University Press.MA: Cambridge.

[24]Lipstz, K.L. 2004. *Campaigns and Competition: How to Enhance Voter Knowledge and   Deliberation in Mass Democracy.* Ph.D. Dissertation, University of California, Berkley, United States.

[25]Freeman, Samuel. 2000. Deliberative Democracy: A Sympathetic Comment. *Philosophy and Public Affair, 29* (4), p.371.

[26]Gomez-Albarello, J.G. 2006. *From an Impartial Vantage Point from Democratic theory to theory of action and vice versa.* Ph.D. Dissertation, Washington University, Washington, United States.

[27]Habermas, J. 1996. *Between Facts and Norms: Contributions to a Discourse Theory of Law and Democracy.* Transl. W. Rehg. Cambridge, MA: MIT Press.

[28]Lipstz, K.L. 2004. *Campaigns and Competition: How to Enhance Voter Knowledge and   Deliberation in Mass Democracy.* Ph.D. Dissertation, University of California, Berkley, United States.

CHAPTER 2

[1]International IDEA (2008). *Assessing the quality of democracy: An overview of the international IDEA framework.* Stockholm: International IDEA.

[2]Ibid.

[3]Bowman, K.S. 1996. Taming the Tiger: Militarization and Democracy in Latin America. *Journal of Peace Research,* Volume *33 (3):* 289-308.

[4]Foweraker, J. and Krznaric, R. 2001. How to construct a database of liberal democratic   performance. *Democratization, 8*(3), 1-25.

[5]Ibid.

[6]Ibid.

[7]Marshall, M.G and Cole, B.R. 2009. Global report 2009.Severn, MD: Center for systemic Peace.

[8]Marshalls, M.G., and Jaggers, K. 2009. *Polity IV project: Political regime characteristics   and transitions, 1800-2009.*Severn, MD: Center for systemic Peace.

[9]Ibid.

[10]International IDEA. 2008. *Assessing the quality of democracy: An overview of the* international IDEA framework. Stockholm: International IDEA.

[11]Ibid.

[12]Bertram, C. 2003. *Rousseau and the social Construct.* London: Routledge.

[13]Asen, R. 2003. The Multiple Mr. Dewey: Multiple Publics and Permeable Borders in   John Dewey's Theory of the Public Sphere. *Argumentation and Advocacy,* 39(3): 174–89.

[14]Roberts, N. 2004. Public Deliberation in an Age of Direct Citizen Participation. *American Review of Public Administration, 34* (4) pp. 315-353.

[15]Kathi, P.C and T. L. Cooper. 2005. Democratizing the Administrative State: Connecting Neighborhood Councils and City Agencies. *Public Administration Review, 65*(5).

[16]Putnam, Roberts. 2000. Bowling Alone: *The collapse and*

Revival of American community. New York: Simon & Schuster.

[17]Kathi, P.C and T. L. Cooper. 2005. Democratizing the Administrative State: Connecting Neighborhood Councils and City Agencies. *Public   Administration Review. 65*(5).

[18]Dahl, R.A. 1989. *Democracy and its Critics.* Connecticut: Yale University Press.

[19]Cooper, T. L. 1983. Citizen Participation. In *Organization Theory and Management*, edited by Thomas D. Lynch, 13– 46. New York: Marcel Dekker.

[20]Marshalls, M.G., and Jaggers, K. 2009. *Polity IV project: Political regime characteristics   and transitions, 1800-2009.*Severn, MD: Center for systemic Peace.

[21]Dahl, R.A. 1989. *Democracy and its Critics.* Connecticut: Yale University Press.

[22]Dahl, R. A. 1966. *Political opposition in Western democracies*. New Haven, CT: Yale University Press.

[23]Shapiro, I. 2003. *The Moral Foundations of Politics*. New Haven: Yale University Press.

[24]LeVan, A. 2007. *Dictators, democrats and development in Nigeria. A PhD Dissertation,* University of California, San Diego.

[25]Alence, R. (2004). Political institutions and development governance in Sub-Saharan Africa. *Journal of Modern African Studies, 42* (2), 163-187.

[26] Satyanath, S; and Subramanian, A. 2004. What determines long-run macroeconomic stability? *IMF Working paper No 04/215*. Retrieved from social science electronic Publishing, Inc.

[27] Alence, R. 2004. Political institutions and development governance in Sub-Saharan Africa. *Journal of Modern African Studies, 42* (2), 163-187.

[28] Marshalls, M.G; and Jaggers, K. 2009. *Polity IV project: Political regime characteristics and transitions, 1800-2009.*Severn, MD: Center for systemic Peace.

[29]Tvinnereim, E. M. 2004. *Democratic contestation, accountability and citizen satisfaction in German states.* Paper presented at the annual Meeting of The Midwest Political Science Association, Palmar House Hilton, Chicago, Illinois.

CHAPTER 3

[1]Buchholz, R. A. 1989. *Business Environment and Public Policy: Implications for Management and Strategy Formulation.*3rd Ed. Englewood Cliffs, New Jersey: Prentice-Hall, Inc.

[2]Ibid.

[3]Anderson, J. E. 2006. *Public Policymaking*. 6th Ed. New York: Houghton Mifflin Company.

[4]Anderson, J.E; D. W. Brady and C. Bullock III. 1978. *Public Policy and Politics in America*. North Scituate, MA: Duxbury.

[5]Ibid.

[6]Lowi, T. J. 1981. *Incomplete Conquest: Governing America,* 2nd Ed. New York: Holt, Rinehart and Winston.

[7]Dye, T. R. 1978. *Understanding Public Policy,* 3rd ed. Englewood Cliffs, NJ: Prentice- Hall.

[8]Buchholz, R. A. 1989. *Business Environment and Public Policy: Implications for Management and Strategy Formulation*.3rd Ed. Englewood Cliffs, New Jersey: Prentice-Hall, Inc.

[9]Ibid.

[10]Anderson, J. E. 2006. *Public Policymaking*. 6th Ed. New York: Houghton Mifflin Company.

[11]Kingdom, J.W. 2003. *Agendas, Alternatives, and Public Policies*. 2nd Ed. New York: Longman.

[12]Buchholz, R. A. 1989. *Business Environment and Public Policy: Implications for Management and Strategy Formulation*. 3rd Ed. Englewood Cliffs, New Jersey: Prentice-Hall, Inc.

[13]Wildavsky, A. 1979. *Speaking Truth to Power: The Art and Craft of Policy Analysis*. Boston, MA: Little Brown.

[14]Patton, C.V; and D.S. Sawicki. 1993. *Basic Methods of Policy Analysis and Planning*.2nd Ed. Englewood Cliffs, New Jersey: Prentice Hall.

[15]Buchholz, R. A. 1989. *Business Environment and Public Policy: Implications for Management and Strategy Formulation*.3rd Ed. Englewood Cliffs, New Jersey: Prentice-Hall, Inc.

[16]Ibid.

[17]Rawls, J. 1971. *.A theory of Justice.* Cambridge, MA: Harvard University Press.

[18]Buchholz, R. A. 1989. *Business Environment and Public Policy: Implications for Management and*

*Strategy Formulation.*3rd Ed. Englewood Cliffs, New Jersey: Prentice-Hall, Inc.

[19]Ibid

[20]Anderson, J.E. 2006. *Public Policymaking.* 6th Ed. New York: Houghton Mifflin Company.

[21]Buchholz, R. A. 1989. *Business Environment and Public Policy: Implications for Management and Strategy Formulation.* 3rd Ed. Englewood Cliffs, New Jersey: Prentice-Hall, Inc.

[22]Ibid.

[23]Ibid.

[24]Ibid.

[25]Ibid.

[26]Anderson, J.E. 2006. *Public Policymaking.* 6th Ed. New York: Houghton Mifflin Company.

[27]Johnson, C. E. 2005. *Meeting the ethical challenges of leadership: Casting light or Shadow.* Thousand Oaks, CA: Sage.

[28]Ibid.

[29]Buchholz, R. A. 1989. *Business Environment and Public Policy: Implications for Management and Strategy Formulation.*3rd Ed. Englewood Cliffs, New Jersey: Prentice-Hall, Inc.

CHAPTER 4

[1]Cooper, T. L; and T.A. Bryer. 2007. William Robertson: Exemplar of Politics and Public Management Rightly Understood. *Public Administration Review, 67* (5), p. 816.

[2]Ibid.

[3]Ibid.

[4] Preston, L.E. and J.E. Post. 1975. *Private Management and Public Policy: The Principle of Public Responsibility.* Englewood Cliffs, NJ: Prentice-Hall, Inc.

[5]Buchholz, R.A. 1989. *Business Environment and Public Policy: Implications for Management and Strategy*

Formulation.3rd Ed. Englewood Cliffs, New Jersey:
Prentice-Hall, Inc.
[6]Anderson, J.E. 2006. *Public Policymaking*. 6th Ed. New
York: Houghton Mifflin Company.
[7]Buchholz, R.A. 1989. *Business Environment and Public
Policy: Implications for Management and Strategy
Formulation*.3rd Ed. Englewood Cliffs, New Jersey:
Prentice-Hall, Inc.
[8]Anderson, J. E. 2006. *Public Policymaking*. 6th Ed. New
York: Houghton Mifflin Company.
[9]Patton, C.V. and D.S. Sawicki. 1993. *Basic Methods of
Policy Analysis and Planning.* 2nd Ed. Englewood Cliffs,
New Jersey: Prentice Hall.
[10]Shafritz, J.M., E. W. Russell, and C. P. Borick. 2007.
Introducing Public Administration. 5thEd.New York:
Pearson-Longman.
[11] Schorr, L.B. 1997. *Common Purpose: Strengthening
Families and Neighborhoods to Rebuild America.* New
York: Anchor Books.
[12]Dunn, W. 2008. *Public Policy Analysis: An
Introduction.* Upper Saddle River, NJ: Pearson Prentice
Hall.

CHAPTER 5

[1]Roberts, N. 2004. Public Deliberation in an Age of
Direct Citizen Participation. *American Review of Public
Administration,* Volume *34* (4) p. 316.
[2]Ibid.
[3]Dahl, R. A. 1989. *Democracy and its Critics*.
Connecticut: Yale University Press.
[4]Kathi, P.C and Cooper, T.L. 2005. Democratizing the
Administrative State: Connecting. Neighborhood
Councils and City Agencies. *Public Administration
Review. 65*(5), p. 560.
[5]Stivers, Camilla. 2008. Public Administration's myth of
Sisyphus. *Administration and Society*, 39(8), 1008-1012.

[6]Ibid.

[7]Kathi, P.C. and T.L. Cooper. 2005. Democratizing the Administrative State: Connecting Neighborhood Councils and City Agencies. *Public Administration Review.* *65*(5).

[8]Asen, R. 2003. The Multiple Mr. Dewey: Multiple Publics and Permeable Borders in   John Dewey's Theory of the Public Sphere. *Argumentation and Advocacy* 39(3): 174–89.

[9] Putnam, Roberts. 2000. *Bowling Alone: The collapse and revival of American community.* New York: Simon & Schuster.

[10]Ibid.

[11]Heyrman, J.P. 1991. *Mobilizing Citizens: A study of citizens' groups and participation.* University of Minnesota, Minnesota, United States.

[12]Irvin, R. A; and Stansbury, J. (2004). Citizen Participation in Decision Making: Is It Worth the Effort? *Public Administration Review 64*(1): 55–65.

[13]King, C. and C. Stiver.1998. *Government Is Us: Public Administration in an Anti-government Era.* Thousand Oaks, CA: Sage Publications.

[14]Kathi, P.C and T.L. Cooper. 2005. Democratizing the Administrative State: Connecting Neighborhood Councils and City Agencies. *Public Administration Review.* *65*(5).

[15]Dachler, H.P., and B. Wilpert. 1978. Conceptual Dimensions and Boundaries of   Participation in Organizations: A Critical Evaluation. *Administrative Science Quarterly* 23(1): 1–39.

[16]John, P. 2009. Can Citizen Governance Redress the Representative Bias of Political Participation? *Public Administration Review.* *69*(3). 494-505.

[17]Kathi, P.C and T.L. Cooper. 2005. Democratizing the Administrative State: Connecting Neighborhood

Councils and City Agencies. *Public Administration Review, 65*(5), p. 559.

[18]Ibid.

[19]Schachter, H.L. 2005 .The Citizen Deliberator. *Public Administration Review.* 65(6)

[20]Fung, A. 2006. Varieties of Participation in Complex Governance. *Public Administration Review,* Volume *66.* Special Issue, pp. 66-75.

[21]Ibid.

[22]Ibid.

[23]Ibid.

[24]Ibid.

[25]Ibid.

[26]Roberts, N. 2004. Public Deliberation in an Age of Direct Citizen Participation. *American Review of Public Administration, 34* (4) pp. 315-353.

[27]Fung, A. 2006. Varieties of Participation in Complex Governance. *Public Administration Review, 66* Special Issue, pp. 66-75.

[28]Ackerman, B; and Fishkin, J.S. 2004. *Deliberation Day.* New Haven, CT: Yale University Press.

[29]Bryer, T. A. 2007. Toward a Relevant Agenda for Responsive Public Administration. *A Journal of Public Administration Research and Theory, 17*(3): 479-500.

[30]Schachter, H.L. 2005 .The Citizen Deliberator. *Public Administration Review, 65*(6).

[31]King, Cheryl S., Kathryn M. Feltey and Bridget O. Susel. 1998. The Question of Participation: Toward Authentic Public Participation in Public Administration. *Public Administration Review*, 58(4): 317-27.

[32]Burtt, S. 1993. The Politics of Virtue Today: A Critique and a Proposal. *American Political Science Review, Volume 87* (2): 360-68.

[33]Ibid.

[34]Booher, D. E. 2004. Collaborative governance practices and democracy. *National Civic Review,* 93(4), 32-46.

[35]Schachter, H.L. 2005 .The Citizen Deliberator. *Public Administration Review,* 65(6).

[36]Booher, D. E. 2004. Collaborative governance practices and democracy. *National Civic Review,* 93(4), 32-46.

[37]Box, R; Marshall, G.S; Reed, B.J; and Reed, C.M. 2001. New Public Management and Substantive Democracy. 2001. *Public Administration Review, 61* (5).

[38]Vigoda, E. 2002. From responsiveness to collaboration: Governance, citizens, and the next generation of public Administration. *Public Administration Review, 62* pp. 527-40.

[39]Vigoda-Gadot, E. 2003. *Managing collaboration in Public Administration: The promise Of Alliance among Governance, citizens and business.* Westport, Ct: Praeger.

[40]Booher, D. E. 2004. Collaborative governance practices and democracy. *National Civic Review,* 93(4), 32-46.

CHAPTER 6

[1]Buchholz, R. A. 1989. *Business Environment and Public Policy: Implications for Management and Strategy Formulation.*3rd Ed. Englewood Cliffs, New Jersey: Prentice-Hall, Inc.

[2]Ibid.

[3]Ibid.

[4]Dye, T. R. 1978. *Understanding Public Policy,* 3rd ed. Englewood Cliffs, NJ: Prentice-Hall, Inc.

[5]Buchholz, R. A. 1989. *Business Environment and Public Policy: Implications for Management and Strategy Formulation.* 3rd Ed. Englewood Cliffs, New Jersey: Prentice-Hall, Inc.

[6]Ibid.

[7]Dye, T.R. 1978. *Understanding Public Policy,* 3rd ed. Englewood Cliffs, NJ: Prentice-Hall, Inc.

[8]Anderson, J.E. 2006. *Public Policymaking*. 6th Ed. New York: Houghton Mifflin Company.

[9]Ibid.

[10]Shafritz, J.M., E. W. Russell, and C.P. Borick. 2007. *Introducing Public Administration.* 5th Ed. New York: Pearson-Longman.

[11]Buchholz, R. A. 1989. *Business Environment and Public Policy: Implications for Management and Strategy Formulation.*3rd Ed. Englewood Cliffs, New Jersey: Prentice-Hall, Inc.

[12]Ibid.

[13]Ibid.

[14]Ibid.

[15]Shafritz, J. M., E. W. Russell, and C.P. Borick. 2007. *Introducing Public Administration.* 5[th]Ed.New York: Pearson-Longman.

[16]Ibid.

[17]Kingdom, J. W. 2003. *Agendas, Alternatives, and Public Policies*. 2nd Ed. New York: Longman.

[18]Patton, C.V; and D. S. Sawicki. 1993. *Basic Methods of Policy Analysis and Planning.* 2nd Ed. Englewood Cliffs, New Jersey: Prentice Hall.

[19]Kingdom, J. W. 2003. *Agendas, Alternatives, and Public Policies*. 2nd Ed. New York: Longman.

CHAPTER 7

[1]Harrison, G. 2008. From the global to the local? Governance and development at the local level: reflections from Tanzania. *Journal of Modern African Studies,* 46, 2 (2008), pp. 169–189.

[2]Ohemeng, F. L. 2005. Getting the State right: think tanks and the dissemination of New Public Management Ideas in Ghana. *Journal of Modern African Studies, 43* (3), pp. 443-465.

[3]Turner, M; and D. Hulme. 1997. Governance, Administration, and Development. Hartford, CT: Kumarian.

[4] Ohemeng, F. L. 2005. Getting the State right: think tanks and the dissemination of New Public Management Ideas in Ghana. *Journal of Modern African Studies, 43* (3), pp. 443-465.

[5]Alence, R. 2004. Political Institutions and Development Governance in Sub-Saharan Africa. *Journal of Modern African Studies,* 42 (2), pp.163-187.

[6] Patton, C.V; and D. S. Sawicki. 1993. *Basic Methods of Policy Analysis and Planning.* 2nd Ed. Englewood Cliffs, New Jersey: Prentice Hall.

[7]Daft, R.L. 1995. *Understanding Management.* New York: The Dryden Press.

CHAPTER 8

[1]USAID Policy. 1991. Democracy and Governance. Washington, DC.

[2]Bowman, K.S. 1996. Taming the Tiger: Militarization and Democracy in Latin America. *Journal of Peace Research, 33 (3):* 289-308.

[3]Satyanath, S. and A. Subramanian. 2004. What Determines Long-Run Macroeconomic Stability? *IMF Working paper No 04/215.*

[4]USAID Policy. 1991. Democracy and Governance. Washington, DC.

[5]Dahl, R.A. 1956. *A Preface to Democratic Theory.* Chicago: The University of Chicago Press.

[6]Williams, E.H. 1996. *Citizen Participation in Administrative Policy Making; Bureaucratic Impediments and Social construction: Implications for Democracy.* Ph. D dissertation, The University of Nebraska, Lincoln, United States.

[7]Olsen, M.E. 1982. *Participatory Pluralism: Political Participation and Influence in*

United States and Sweden. Chicago: Nelson-Hall.
[8]Renn, et al. 1993. Public Participation in Decision-making: A three-Step Process. *Policy Sciences, 26*(3) 189-214.
[9]Laudon, K. 1977. *Communications Technology and Democratic Participation.* New York: Praeger Publishers.
[10]Olsen, M. E. 1982. *Participatory Pluralism: Political Participation and Influence in United States and Sweden.* Chicago: Nelson-Hall.
[11]Williams, E. H. 1996. *Citizen Participation in Administrative Policy Making; Bureaucratic Impediments and Social construction: Implications for Democracy.* Ph. D. Dissertation. The University of Nebraska, Lincoln, United States.
[12]Ibid.
[13]Manin, B. 1997. *The Principles of Representative Government.* UK: Cambridge University Press.
[14]Roberts, N. 2004. Public Deliberation in an Age of Direct Citizen Participation. *American Review of Public Administration, 34* (4) pp.315-353.
[15]Ibid.
[16]USAID Policy. 1991. Democracy and Governance. Washington, DC.
[17]Satyanath, S; and A. Subramanian. 2004. What Determines Long-Run Macroeconomic Stability? *IMF Working paper No 04/215.*
[18]Roberts, N. 2004. Public Deliberation in an Age of Direct Citizen Participation. *American Review of Public Administration, 34* (4) pp. 315-353.
[19]Williams, E. H. 1996. *Citizen Participation in Administrative Policy Making; Bureaucratic Impediments and Social construction: Implications for Democracy.* Ph. D dissertation, The University of Nebraska, Lincoln, United States.
[20]Ibid.

[21]Ibid.

[22]Orosco, J.A. (2002) *Strong Democratic Vistas: Deliberative and Participatory in Twentieth Century American Philosophy.* Ph.D. Dissertation. University of California, Riverside, United States.

[23]Ibid.

[24]Ibid.

[25]Habermas, J. 1984. *The Theory of Communicative Action. Volume 1: Reason and the Rationalization of Society.* Boston, MA: Beacon.

[26]Gomez-Albarello, J.G. 2006. *From an Impartial Vantage Point from Democratic theory to theory of action and vice versa.* Ph.D. Dissertation. Washington University. Washington, United States.

[27]Ibid.

CHAPTER 9

[1]Boyte, H.C. 2005. Reframing Democracy: Governance, Civic Agency, and Politics. *Public Administration Review.* 65(5).

[2]Ibid.

[3]Ibid.

[4]Bingham, L. B; and T. Nabatchi. 2005. The New Governance: Practices and Processes for Stakeholder and Citizen Participation in the Work of Government. *Public Administration Review. 65*(5).

[5]Ibid.

[6]Ibid.

[7]Ibid.

[8]Ibid.

[9]Ibid.

[10]Feng, Y. 2005. *Democracy, governance, and economic performance: Theory and evidence.* Cambridge, MA: The MIT press.

[11]Boix, C. 2003. *Democracy and redistribution.* Cambridge, MA; Cambridge University Press.

[12]Brown, W. 2006. The Commission for Africa: results and prospects for the West's Africa policy. *Journal of Modern African Studies, 44* (3), pp. 349–374.

[13]USAID Policy. (1991. Democracy and Governance. Washington, DC.

[14]Ibid.

[15]Alence, R. 2004. Political Institutions and Development Governance in Sub-Saharan Africa. *Journal of Modern African Studies,* 42 (2), pp. 163-187.

[16]Ibid.

[17]Brinkman, R. L. 1995. Economic Growth versus Economic Development: Towards a Conceptual Clarification. *Journal of Economic Issues*, 29(4), pp.1171-1188.

[18]Hosseini, H. (2003).Why Development is more complex Than Growth: clarifying some confusions. *Review of social economy*, LXI (1), pp. 93-110.

[19]Chen, E.K.Y. 2005. Teaching and Learning Development Economics: Retrospect and Prospect. *Journal of Economic Education,* 36(3).

[20]Wang, J. 2009. Some Reflections on Modernization Theory and Globalization Theory. *Chinese Studies in History,* 43 (1), pp.72-98.

[21]Cao, F. 2009. Modernization Theory and China's Road to Modernization. *Chinese studies in History,* 43(1).

[22]Ibid.

[23]Ibid.

[24]Organski, A. F. K. 1973. *The Stages of Political Development.* New York: Alfred A. Knopt.

[25] Cao, F. 2009. Modernization Theory and China's Road to Modernization. *Chinese studies in History,* 43(1).

[26]Ibid.

[27]Shie, V.H. & Meer, C. D. 2010.The Rise of Knowledge in Dependency Theory: The Experience of India and

Taiwan. *Review of Radical Political Economics,* 42(1), pp.81-99.
[28]Cao, F. 2009. Modernization Theory and China's Road to Modernization. *Chinese studies in History,* 43(1).

CHAPTER 10

[1]Shafritz, J.M., Russell, E.W; and Borick, C.P. 2007. *Introducing Public Administration.* 5[th]Ed. New York: Pearson-Longman.
[2]Ibid.
[3]Anderson, J.E. 2006. *Public Policymaking.* 6th Ed. New York: Houghton Mifflin Company.
[4]Kelleher, C; and S. W. Yackee. 2004. An Empirical Assessment on Devolution's Policy Impact. *The Policy Studies Journal, 32*(2).

CHAPTER 11

[1]Cooper, T. L; and T. A. Bryer. 2007. William Robertson: Exemplar of Politics and Public Management Rightly Understood. *Public Administration Review. 67* (5), p.816.
[2]Ibid.
[3]Ibid.
[4]John, P. 2009. Can Citizen Governance Redress the Representative Bias of Political Participation? *Public Administration Review. 69*(3), 494-505.
[5]Fung, A. 2006. Varieties of Participation in Complex Governance. *Public Administration Review, 66.*Special Issue, pp. 66-75.
[6]Dahl, R. A. 1953. *On Democracy.* New Haven, CT: Yale University Press.
[7]John, P. 2009. Can Citizen Governance Redress the Representative Bias of Political Participation? *Public Administration Review, 69*(3). 494-505.

[8]Box, R.C. 1998. *Citizen Governance: Leading American Communities Into the 21st Century.* Thousand Oaks, CA: Sage Publications.

[9]Dahl, R.A. 1989. *Democracy and its Critics.* Connecticut: Yale University Press.

[10]Cooper, T. L. 1983. Citizen Participation. In *Organization Theory and Management*, edited by Thomas D. Lynch, 13– 46. New York: Marcel Dekker.

[11]Roberts, N. 2004. Public Deliberation in an Age of Direct Citizen Participation. *American Review of Public Administration, 34* (4) pp. 315-353.

[12]Bryer, T. A. 2007. Toward a Relevant Agenda for Responsive Public Administration. *A Journal of Public Administration Research and Theory, 17*(3): 479-500.

[13]Roberts, N. 2004. Public Deliberation in an Age of Direct Citizen Participation. *American Review of Public Administration, 34* (4) pp.315-353.

[14]Bingham, L. B; and T. Nabatchi. 2005. The New Governance: Practices and Processes for Stakeholder and Citizen Participation in the Work of Government. *Public Administration Review, 65*(5).

[15]Ibid.

[16]Ibid.

CHAPTER 12

[1]Boyte, H.C. 2005. Reframing Democracy: Governance, Civic Agency, and Politics. *Public Administration Review, 65*(5).

[2]Ibid.

[3]Ibid.

[4]Ibid.

[5]Stivers, Camilla. 1999, p. 88. Translating Out of Time: Public Administration and Its History. *Public Administration Review, 59* (4): 362-67.

[6]Roberts, N. 2004. Public Deliberation in an Age of Direct Citizen Participation. *American Review of Public Administration, 34* (4) pp. 315-353.

[7]Putnam, Roberts. 2000. *Bowling Alone: The collapse and revival of American community.* New York: Simon & Schuster.

[8]Sandel, Michael. 1998. Democracy's Discontent: America in Search of Public Philosophy. Boston, MA: Harvard University Press.

[9]Denhardt, R. B., and J. V. Denhardt. 2000, p. 552. The New Public Service: Serving Rather than Steering. *Public Administration Review, 60*(6): 549–60.

[10]Sandel, Michael. 1998. *Democracy's Discontent: America in Search of Public Philosophy.* Boston, MA: Harvard University Press.

[11] Stivers, Camilla. 1999, p. 88. Translating Out of Time: Public Administration and Its History. *Public Administration Review,* 59 (4): 362-67.

[12]Vigoda, E. 2002. From responsiveness to collaboration: Governance, citizens, and the next generation of public Administration. *Public Administration Review, 62* pp. 527-40.

[13]Bingham, L.B; and T. Nabatchi. 2005. The New Governance: Practices and Processes for Stakeholder and Citizen Participation in the Work of Government. *Public Administration Review. 65*(5).

[14]Ibid, p. 550.

[15]King, C; and C. Stivers. 1998. *Government Is Us: Public Administration in an Anti- government Era.* Thousand Oaks, CA: Sage Publications.

[16]Bingham, L.B; and T. Nabatchi. 2005. The New Governance: Practices and Processes for Stakeholder and Citizen Participation in the Work of Government. *Public Administration Review. 65*(5).

[17]Denhardt, R. B., and J.V. Denhardt. 2000. The New Public Service: Serving Rather than Steering. *Public Administration Review 60*(6): 549–60.

[18]Bingham, L.B. and T. Nabatchi, T. 2005. The New Governance: Practices and Processes for Stakeholder and

Citizen Participation in the Work of Government. *Public Administration Review. 65*(5).
[19]Ibid, p. 550.
[20]Ibid.
[21]Ibid, p. 554.
[22]Ibid, p. 547.

CHAPTER 13

[1]Booher, D. E. 2004. Collaborative governance practices and democracy. *National   Civic Review,* 93(4), 32-46.
[2]Ibid.
[3]Koteen, J. 1997. *Strategic Management in Public and Nonprofit Organizations: Managing Public Concerns in an Era of Limits.* Westport; Connecticut: Praeger.
[4]Ibid.
[5]Kemmelmeier, M., et al. 2003. Individualism, Collectivism, and Authoritarianism in Seven Societies. *Journal of Cross-Cultural Psychology, 34* (3): 304-322.
[6] Wood, A. 2007. Cross-cultural moral philosophy: reflections on Thaddeus Metz: "Toward an African moral theory." *South African Journal of Philosophy.* 26, 4: 336-346
[7]Ibid.
[8]Riccucci, Norma M. 2009, p. 373). The Pursuit of Social Equity in the Federal Government: A road Less Traveled. Public Administration Review 69(3): 373- 82.
[9]Ibid.
[10]Ibid.
[11]Ibid.
[12]West, J. and E. Berman 2006. *The Ethics Edge.* 2nd Edition. City Council Management. Association. Washington D.C.
[13]Stoner, J.A. & Freeman, R.E. 1989. *Management.* New Jersey: Prentice-Hill.

[14]West, J. and E. Berman. 2006. *The Ethics Edge.* 2nd Edition. City Council Management Association. Washington D.C.

[15]Berman, E.M., West, J.P; and Bonczek, S.J. (1998). *The Ethics Edge. International City/County Management Association.* Washington D.C.

[16]Swaidan, Z; Vitell, S.J; Rawwas, Y.A. (August, 2003). Consumer Ethics: Determinants of Ethical Beliefs of African Americans. *Journal of Business Ethics,* 46, 2, p. 177.

[17]Anderson, J. E. 2006. *Public Policymaking.* 6th Ed. New York: Houghton Mifflin Company.

CHAPTER 14

[1]Bryce, H. J. 2006. Nonprofits as social capital and agents in the public policy process: Toward a new paradigm. *Nonprofit & Voluntary Sector Quarterly,* 35(2), 311-318.

[2]Bingham, L. B; and T. Nabatchi. 2005, p. 554. The New Governance: Practices and Processes for Stakeholder and Citizen Participation in the Work of Government. *Public Administration Review, 65*(5).

[3]Ibid, p. 550.

[4]Fung, A. 2003. Associations and Democracy: Between Theories, Hopes and Realities. *Annual Review of Sociology, 29*(1), 515-539.

[5]Chambers, S. and W. Kymlicka. 2002. *Alternative Conceptions of Civil Society.* Princeton, NJ: Princeton University Press.

[6]Fung, A. 2003. Associations and Democracy: Between Theories, Hopes and Realities. *Annual Review of Sociology, 29*(1), 515-539.

[7]Ibid.

[8]Verba, S; K. L. Schlozman, and H. E. Brady. 1995. *Voice and Equality: Civic Voluntarism in American Politics.* Cambridge, MA: Harvard University Press.

[9]Fung, A. 2003, p.517. Associations and Democracy: Between Theories, Hopes and Realities. *Annual Review of Sociology, 29*(1), 515-539.
[10]Ibid, p. 518.
[11]Ibid, p. 518.
[12]Ibid, p. 522.
[13]Ibid, p. 518.
[14]Ibid, p. 523.
[15]Ibid, p. 530.
[16]Heyrman, J. P. 1991. *Mobilizing Citizens: A study of citizens' groups and participation.* University of Minnesota, Minnesota, United States.
[17] Berry, J. 1977. *Lobbying for the people.* Princeton, NJ: Princeton University
[18]Heyrman, J. P. 1991. *Mobilizing Citizens: A study of citizens' groups and participation.* University of Minnesota, Minnesota, United States.
[19]Kathi, P. C., and T. L. Cooper. 2005. Democratizing the Administrative State: Connecting Neighborhood Councils and City Agencies. *Public Administration Review. 65*(5).
[20]Irvin, R. A. and J. Stansbury. 2004. Citizen Participation in Decision Making: Is It Worth the Effort? *Public Administration Review 64*(1): 55–65.
[21]Alford, J. 2002. Why Do Public-Sector Clients Coproduce? Toward a Contingency Theory. *Administration and Society* 34(1): 32–47.
[22]Kathi, P.C; and T. L. Cooper. 2005. Democratizing the Administrative State: Connecting Neighborhood Councils and City Agencies. *Public Administration Review. 65*(5).
[23]Weber, Edward P. 1998. A Wish List for 21st Century Environmental Policy: Decentralization, Integration, Cooperation, Flexibility, and Enhanced Participation by Citizens and Local Governments. *Policy Studies Journal, 26*(1): 185–96.

[24]Bingham, L.B. and T. Nabatchi. 2005. The New Governance: Practices and Processes for Stakeholder and Citizen Participation in the Work of Government. *Public Administration Review.* *65*(5).

[25]Asen, R. 2003. The Multiple Mr. Dewey: Multiple Publics and Permeable Borders in John Dewey's Theory of the Public Sphere. *Argumentation and Advocacy* 39(3): 174–89.

[26]Bingham, L. B. and T. Nabatchi. 2005. The New Governance: Practices and Processes for Stakeholder and Citizen Participation in the Work of Government. *Public Administration Review.* *65*(5).

CHAPTER 15

[1]Asen, R. 2003. The Multiple Mr. Dewey: Multiple Publics and Permeable Borders in John Dewey's Theory of the Public Sphere. *Argumentation and Advocacy,* 39(3): 174–89.

[2]Cohen, J. and J. Rogers. In Fung, A. 2003. Associations and Democracy: Between Theories, Hopes and Realities. Annual Review of Sociology, 29, pp. 515-39.

[3]Bierschenk, T. 2006. The local appropriation of democracy: an analysis of the Municipal elections in Parakou, Republic of Benin, 2002 –03. *Journal of Modern African Studies, 44*, 4 (2006), pp. 543–571.

[4]Ibid.

[5]Ibid.

[6]Ibid.

[7]Alence, R. 2004. Political Institutions and Development Governance in Sub-Saharan Africa. *Journal of Modern African Studies,* 42 (2), pp. 163-187.

[8]Fung, A. 2003. Associations and Democracy: Between Theories, Hopes and Realities. *Annual Review of Sociology, 29*(1), 515-539.

[9]Irvin, R. A; and J. Stansbury. 2004. Citizen Participation in Decision Making: Is It Worth the Effort? *Public Administration Review 64*(1): 55–65.

[10]Bingham, L.B. and T. Nabatchi. 2005. The New Governance: Practices and Processes for Stakeholder and Citizen Participation in the Work of Government. *Public Administration Review. 65*(5).

[11]Asen, R. 2003. The Multiple Mr. Dewey: Multiple Publics and Permeable Borders in John Dewey's Theory of the Public Sphere. *Argumentation and Advocacy,* 39(3): 174–89.

[12]Bingham, L.B. and T. Nabatchi. 2005. The New Governance: Practices and Processes for Stakeholder and Citizen Participation in the Work of Government. *Public Administration Review. 65*(5).

[13]Kamensky, J.M; and T. J. Burlin. *Collaboration: Using Networks and Partnerships.* New York: Rowman & Littlefield Publishers.

[14]Box, R; Marshall, G.S; Reed, B.J; and Reed, C.M. (2001). New Public Management and Substantive Democracy. 2001. *Public Administration Review. 61* (5).

[15]Booher, D. E. 2004. Collaborative governance practices and democracy. *National Civic Review,* 93(4), 32-46.

[16]John, P. 2009. Can Citizen Governance Redress the Representative Bias of Political Participation? *Public Administration Review. 69*(3). 494-505.

[17]Cooper, T.L., and T. A. Bryer. 2007. William Robertson: Exemplar of Politics and Public Management Rightly Understood. *Public Administration Review. 67(*5), p. 816.

[18]Booher, D. E. 2004. Collaborative governance practices and democracy. *National Civic Review,* 93(4), 32-46.

CHAPTER 16

[1]Koteen, J. 1997. *Strategic Management in Public and Nonprofit Organizations: Managing Public Concerns in an Era of Limits.* Westport; Connecticut: Praeger.

[2]Gordon, G. L. 2005. *Strategic planning for local government.* Washington, DC: International City/County Management Association (ICMA).

[3]Kingdom, J.W. 2003. *Agendas, Alternatives, and Public Policies.* 2nd Ed. New York: Longman.

[4]Gordon, G. L. 2005. *Strategic planning for local government.* Washington, DC: International City/County Management Association (ICMA).

[5]Center for Public Productivity. 2005. *A Brief guide to productivity performance.* NJ: Rutgers University.

[6] Ibid.

[7]Daft, R.L. 1995. Understanding Management. New York: The Dryden Press.

[8]Center for Public Productivity. 2005. A Brief guide to productivity performance. NJ: Rutgers University.

9Ibid.

[10]Koteen, J. 1997. Strategic Management in Public and Nonprofit Organizations: Managing Public Concerns in an Era of Limits. Westport; Connecticut: Praeger.

[12]Gordon, G. L. 2005. Strategic planning for local government. Washington, DC: International City/County Management Association (ICMA).

[13]Ibid.

www.ingramcontent.com/pod-product-compliance
Lightning Source LLC
Chambersburg PA
CBHW050348280326
41933CB00010BA/1379